ADEPTUS CUSTODES

THE GOLDEN LEGION

CONTENTS

PRODUCED BY GAMES WORKSHOP IN NOTTINGHAM

For Alan Bligh

With thanks to the Mournival for their additional playtesting services

Games Workshop Ltd, Willow Rd, Lenton, Nottingham, NG7 2WS
games-workshop.com

INTRODUCTION

This grand volume of Imperial lore concerns itself with the proud and storied organisation known as the Adeptus Custodes. The content within will help you to assemble your collection of Adeptus Custodes Citadel Miniatures into a redoubtable tabletop army, ready to take the fight to the heretic, traitor and alien alike in the glorious name of the Emperor of Mankind.

The Adeptus Custodes are Humanity's greatest warriors. They are demigods clad in armour of gleaming auramite, who wield the Imperium's deadliest and most finely crafted weapons. Theirs is a singular duty, perhaps the most important in all the galaxy, for it is to the Adeptus Custodes that the safety and sanctity of the Emperor himself is entrusted. For many thousands of years this has seen them guard the Sol System with ironclad determination, and fight secret wars of which the wider Imperium can never know. But now, with the immaterium spilling through the bounds of reality and war consuming every Imperial world, the Custodians must strike out into the stars to eliminate terrible dangers before they can come anywhere near their throne-bound master. In collecting an Adeptus Custodes army you will find yourself leading the most elite military branch of the Imperium. Every warrior you command is a figure worthy of legend. Every blow you strike will be crushing. Marshal your forces well, for they are few, but know that even a handful of the Emperor's praetorians can seize victory over an entire army of foes.

As well as being incredibly powerful on the tabletop, the Adeptus Custodes are a wonderful modelling and painting project for those who really enjoy lavishing time and attention on every model. With a small number of exquisitely detailed individual warriors and ornate war machines at your disposal, you can afford to spend as long as you wish making sure that every single model in your collection looks exceptional, both by itself and as part of a wider tabletop force.

Within this book you will find all the information you need to collect an Adeptus Custodes army and field it upon the tabletop.

BROTHERHOOD OF DEMIGODS: This section gives an insight into who the Adeptus Custodes are, how they are created, and the noble yet tragic battles that they have fought for ten thousand years, along with examples of how they are assembled for battle.

THE SPLENDOUR OF HOLY TERRA: Here you will find a showcase of beautifully painted Citadel Miniatures that display the varying panoply and resplendent iconography of the Adeptus Custodes, as well as example armies to inspire your own collection.

THE ARMY OF TERRA: This section includes datasheets, wargear lists and weapon rules for every Adeptus Custodes unit, allowing you to field them in your games of Warhammer 40,000.

AURIC MORTALIS: This section provides additional rules – including Warlord Traits, Stratagems, Relics, and matched play points – that allow you to transform your collection of Citadel Miniatures into a magnificent Adeptus Custodes shield host.

To play games with your army, you will need a copy of the Warhammer 40,000 rules. To find out more about Warhammer 40,000 or download the free core rules, visit warhammer40000.com.

They charged into battle like demigods, magnificent warriors seemingly stepped straight from a fresco on a cathedrum wall. The light of the Emperor shone from them like the radiance of Sol herself, and their battle cry was the booming voice of the Master of Mankind. Before their glorious charge, the worshippers of the Dark Gods were driven back like whipped curs.

BROTHERHOOD OF DEMIGODS

The Adeptus Custodes are the Emperor's personal guard. For ten millennia they have stood sentinel over the Master of Mankind and defended the gates of his palace. Yet now the Emperor's blades are unsheathed. The Ten Thousand walk the stars in numbers not seen since the Great Crusade, and woe betide those who oppose them.

No finer or more fearsome warriors are there in the Imperium than the Custodians. Biochemically fashioned from infancy to function as supreme combatants, tacticians and bodyguards, they are death incarnate to those who defy the Emperor's will.

Each Custodian is sublimely skilled, their strategic and tactical nous, bladesmanship and instinct little short of supernatural. They are to the Emperor's Space Marines what those transhuman warriors are to unaugmented Imperial soldiery, an elevated elite whose raw strength and willpower are wholly insurmountable. However, where the warriors of the Adeptus Astartes employ squad-level tactics, their battle-brothers functioning as a cohesive whole, the Custodians fight as individuals. Each of their fiercely independent number wields weapons hand crafted for him alone, and wears intricately designed armour tailored to his precise dimensions. So equipped, a single Custodian can go toe to toe with a dozen experienced combatants. When deployed en masse, such warriors can sweep away armies many times their number.

Where the gilded shield companies of the Adeptus Custodes storm into battle, the enemies of the Emperor come apart like smoke in a gale. The Custodians fight like legends come to life, and with the range of tools at their disposal are able to achieve the impossible. Enemy engines of war are annihilated by swift-striking spearheads of airborne Vertus Praetors, while heretical demagogues and roaring monstrosities alike fall beneath the blades of the Allarus Terminators.

By the time the foe realise their cause is hopeless, it is far too late. The Emperor's praetorians have butchered their leaders, reduced their machines to scrap and cut a path to the very heart of their ranks. The only option left to the enemy to flee in dismay, and even then death is all but guaranteed. Such is the fate of those who dare to oppose the will of the Emperor.

Though even a small force of Custodians can rip through an enemy army in a whirlwind of bloodied blades, their true purpose is not one of conquest, but of guardianship. The Custodians are the Emperor's personal guard, his Ten Thousand, and since time immemorial their role has been to protect their master from harm.

It was at the nadir of the period known as Old Night that the Emperor arose on Terra. The cradle world was, at that time, a nightmarish place of abhuman armies and grotesque warlords who fought in thrall to entities both malefic and debased. What records survive of that terrible age are rightly locked away within the deepest vaults of the Emperor's palace. Were some brave scholar to somehow delve into those ancient histories, they would find that even the earliest sources concerning the Emperor's deeds had him flanked by warriors tall and mighty, who wore plumed helms and carried spears of gold. Through all the horrors of the Unification Wars, through the doomed rebellion of the Thunder Warriors and the establishment of the nascent Imperium, and on into the sweeping conquests of the Great Crusade, the Adeptus Custodes were ever the Emperor's blades. It is said that to have seen the Master of Mankind stride to war at the head of the Golden Legion was to have witnessed the most magnificent spectacle in human history.

For years uncounted the Legio Custodes, as they were known then, covered themselves in glory. Led by the peerless Captain-General Constantin Valdor, they were an unstoppable force, and even during the civil strife of the Horus Heresy they remained utterly resolute and unquestionably loyal, feted throughout the Imperium as the Emperor's finest warriors. Yet it was at the culmination of that epochal conflict that the Custodians knew defeat at last. When Warmaster Horus struck down the Emperor, the Adeptus Custodes failed in their sworn duty. They have carried the crushing shame and dishonour of doing so with them through all the millennia since.

> '*Ours is the duty absolute. Ours is the vigil that must never end. Ours is the timeless honour, the willing sacrifice, the penitence enduring. We stand a watch that will never be relieved, and we stand it gladly out of adoration for he who gave us life, and whose life we must, in turn, preserve. We will never earn absolution, for we do not deserve it, but those who believe that would give us pause are fools.*'
>
> *- Shield-Captain Tybalus Maxin*

In the wake of the Heresy, the Legio Custodes became the Adeptus Custodes. No longer would they fight at their master's side, for the Emperor was little more than a shattered cadaver, his potent will kept alive by the machineries of the Golden Throne. Now, instead, the Custodians were charged with protecting what remained of their beloved Emperor at any cost. They donned shrouds of mourning black as a symbol of their disgrace, a sombre raiment that they would not shed for many millennia.

For thousands of years, the Adeptus Custodes have stood vigil. Thanks to the remarkable gene-craft involved in their creation, these warriors do not age as other men, and so barring catastrophic physical trauma, they are functionally immortal. With many Custodians being well over one thousand years old, they have had endless opportunity to perfect their skills, further their education across every lore and discipline, and hone their tactics so as to be ready for every eventuality.

Through the rituals known as Blood Games the Adeptus Custodes have endlessly tested Terra's defences, despatching their own warriors under hidden aliases to test every route of attack and attempt to breach the walls and gates that protect the Golden Throne. At the same time, the Custodians have utilised fractal thought exercises, centuries-long strategic cogitations and elaborate hallucinarium mock conflicts to perfect their tactics should such a time come that they were released to fight across the Emperor's realm again. Now, with the awakening of the Ultramarines Primarch Roboute Guilliman and his reinstating as Lord Commander of the Imperium, and the opening of the apocalyptic Great Rift, that time has finally come.

Chaos-worshipping Renegades and howling tides of Daemons spill from warp storms all across the galaxy. Even the Sol System is assailed, the greatest enemies of Mankind coming within striking distance of Holy Terra itself. It has become increasingly clear that the Adeptus Custodes can no longer afford to stand silent vigil over the Emperor's palace while the wider Imperium burns around it, the fires of war drawing closer to them by the day. The threats to the Golden Throne are now so widespread and dire that they must be stamped out pre-emptively, before they have a chance to fully manifest.

Thus, while a standing garrison of Custodians remain upon the throneworld to defend their master, dozens of shield companies have set out into the stars to take the fight directly to those who would once again prove them derelict in their duty. With them they bring the fury of the Emperor himself, sharpened by ten thousand years of preparation.

Of course, this is not the only war that the Adeptus Custodes have mobilised for since the Heresy. Were the common herd of Humanity to learn of the clandestine campaigns that the Emperor's guardians have fought upon Terra and beyond, they would doubtless be driven mad with terror. The Custodians have held back the deadly denizens of rune-locked vaults deep beneath the Himalayic Shelf, launched missions into sub-realities seething with horror, purged cults amongst the endless tunnels of Manufactora Mericum, and slain the followers of ultra-radical Inquisitors convinced that the Emperor's final ascension can come only in death. Such battles grind on even as the Ten Thousand sweep out to rend the traitor and the heretic all across known space. Like the Imperium as a whole, the Adeptus Custodes face opposition on every front.

Upon the killing fields of Hydraphur, the Black Legion advanced in great and fearsome number. Yet though the heretics put all other Imperial servants to flight, they could not overcome the Adeptus Custodes, and against that living bastion of auramite their charge broke.

'For one hundred years I stood my watch amidst the sombre shadows of the Sanctum Imperialis. I was still as a statue, but always ready, always attuned to dangers unseen. Days, months, years passed by in a frenzied blur beyond those walls, yet within, little moved and nothing changed. For one hundred years I did naught but wait, yet had any threat appeared, I would have struck it down in a heartbeat. For one hundred years I stood my watch, and as it ends I can tell you this – patience is a weapon.'

- Custodian Warden Tybaris Constor

BODYGUARDS OF THE EMPEROR

The origins of the Adeptus Custodes lie buried in Humanity's obscured past, their secrets bound inseparably to those of the Emperor himself.

During the Dark Age of Technology, the human race was almost annihilated by its own hubris. Though Mankind's first steps away from its home world were faltering, natural adaptability and belligerence of spirit soon saw it flourish in the void. Science and technology advanced at a breathtaking pace, enabling the conquest of increasingly far-flung planets. The vast reaches of the galaxy shrank as Mankind's capabilities grew, and alien races were driven back into the shadows by the fierce light of human progress.

Thinking machines and the development of ever more esoteric weapons and transportation technologies played their part, but the single greatest factor to drive this expansion was the ability – and the reckless will – to manipulate human genetics. Utterly certain of their own primacy, scientist-kings and techno-demagogues followed every strand of curiosity and exercised powers of creation that made them seem like gods. Ultimately, their hubris led them to catastrophe, and onwards to the very brink of extinction. Worlds were overrun by bloody uprisings within their own populations, much of which were mutated beyond sanity and recognition. Gene-wars consumed entire star systems, while a psychic apocalypse drowned the stars in fire. The vast empire of Humanity was shattered amidst horror and anarchy, and the oppressive shroud of Old Night settled over all.

At the heart of this galactic disaster lay Terra, transformed from a glittering jewel to an apocalyptic hellscape by forbidden weapons and biological atrocities. Yet though its people fell into darkness and ignorance, many of the technologies that had led them to ruin survived, sealed away in hidden bunkers and biomantic crypts. Sure enough, as Humanity clawed its way back from the brink beneath the lashes of cruel warlords, so those self-appointed rulers discovered the weapons of old and tried once again to turn them upon one another. Terra faced the threat of a second apocalypse as gene-bred barbarians and ghastly flesh-stitched ghouls made war at the behest of madmen, fanatics and techno-cannibalistic murderers.

Much of this lore is lost forever, destroyed or buried in the endless archives of Terra. Yet a few still know that this was the environment in which the Emperor rose to prominence, and that he – whether living deity or apex superhuman – was a worthy inheritor to the trove of genetomantic lore left behind by Mankind's former rulers. It was this ancient and dangerous bounty, coupled with his own incredible and unfathomable powers, that allowed the Emperor to fashion warriors with which to unite a world.

That task was not a simple one, and though the Emperor sought peace for Humanity, he could not achieve his aims without war. It is known, by the most learned of Imperial Historitors, that the living weapons the Emperor used for his early conquests were the Thunder Warriors. Techno-barbarians transformed into powerful, but ultimately flawed and short-lived, super-soldiers, the Thunder

Legions were fit for a single purpose, after which the Emperor's use for them was done. By the time the Thunder Warriors learned of their own disposable nature, the Emperor had set his sights on grander ambitions, and created the first of the beings that would become his Space Marines.

Not even the most knowledgeable of the Imperium's scholars can say when the Emperor fashioned the Custodians. The truth is hidden in fragments of the past, accounts of figures appearing in crude hieroglyphs and cave etchings, stasis-locked scads of parchment and gene-sealed tomes that no man now can open. They speak of the towering demigods that strode at the Emperor's side, trusted bodyguards and respected counsellors that he took into his confidence. Custodians fought alongside their master before the walls of the Vilifactor's fortress. They held back the baying flesh-packs of the transnordic reaver tribes while the Emperor slew their bloated meat-god. Custodian blades took the head of Gharsha the Decryer, pierced the heart of the Ur-queen of Atlan, and drove back the iron fiends on the red fields of Primasalia. Or at least, so the dying echoes of history suggest.

In the last years of the Unification Wars, the Thunder Warriors at last realised that their creator had cursed them with short lifespans, and turned upon him for what they saw as his betrayal. It was a cadre of several hundred Custodians, even then believed to have been led by the legendary Constantin Valdor, that stood in the Emperor's defence, carrying out a merciless culling of the obsolete and rebellious gene-soldiers. With those last relic forces purged in a ruthless act of barbarity worthy of culminating the Age of Strife, Terra could at last be pronounced unified, and the Emperor could turn his gaze to the stars for the benefit of all Mankind.

The years that followed saw the Great Crusade surge forth from the cradle of Humanity to reclaim the galaxy. First the Sol System was secured, and Mars brought back into the fold through the Emperor's diplomacy and wisdom. Gathering pace with the technological aid of the Martian Mechanicum, the crusade forces spilled out into the void, billions upon billions of Imperial Army soldiers, proud warships, Space Marine Legions and countless other forces setting sail to reunite the stellar empire of Mankind.

In those early days the Emperor was at the forefront of the expansion, even as his Primarch sons were rediscovered one by one and the crusade fleets became ever more scattered and autonomous in their operation. Wherever the Emperor went, there too strode the Legio Custodes, an unstoppable golden army now ten thousand strong. To them went the finest weapons and armour, and all the accumulated wealth of archeotechnological secrets unearthed by the crusading armies upon ancient human worlds. Alongside such esoterica as anti-gravitic battle tanks and terrifyingly potent disintegration rays, the Custodians also had access to the very best tried-and-tested Imperial tools of war. Their Land Raiders possessed the most exceptional and bellicose machine spirits. Their bolt weaponry, power blades and heavy weapons were all individually handcrafted by the greatest artisans the Imperium had to offer, as befitted such august and sublimely skilled warriors.

From the hellish fastness of the Styxian Overmancers to the false empire of the Pureblood Kings, the bitter battles of the Coldharvest Campaign to the triumphant conquest of Ullanor, the Legio Custodes fought undefeated at the Emperor's side. Led to war by the Master of Mankind himself, they were the bane of every foe. Yet they would soon face their sternest and most tragic test.

It is said that the golden-armoured giants of the Legio Custodes were the right hand of the Emperor, while the eerie witch-hunting nulls of the Silent Sisterhood were his left. Together they represent the Talons of the Emperor.

THE HORUS HERESY

Humanity's preeminent destiny seemed assured beneath the Emperor's rule, but it was not to be. In an act of grossest betrayal, fully half of the Space Marine Primarchs turned against their father and began a civil war more ferocious than anything Mankind had ever endured. This was the Horus Heresy, and it would see tragedy wrought on a galactic scale.

The Primarchs were the pinnacle of the Emperor's gene-craft, alchemically fashioned demigods intended to lead his wars of reconquest across the stars. By the machinations of the Dark Gods of Chaos, they were scattered across the cosmos before they had fully formed, and so were reunited with their father – and the Space Marine Legions made in their image – piecemeal as the Great Crusade came to the worlds upon which they had fallen.

Arguably the greatest of their number was Horus Lupercal. It was he whom the Emperor and his Custodians found first, and who fought at his father's side at the head of his Legion, the Luna Wolves. It was Horus whom the Emperor named Warmaster in the wake of the Triumph at Ullanor, charging his gene-son with commanding the Great Crusade in his stead while he and his Custodians returned to Terra to complete new and secret works.

Despite his potential it was Horus, too, who fell to the lure of the Dark Gods, who was utterly corrupted by their touch, and who led fully half of his brothers into damnation along with him. The tragic events of the Horus Heresy – a full account of which would take more than a lifetime to relate – were cataclysmic in the extreme, sundering the nascent Imperium and leaving it to burn in the fires of treachery. It is notable that while the Space Marine Legions battled furiously against one another – and the Imperial Army and Mechanicum tore themselves to shreds with internecine conflict – the Legio Custodes were strangely absent for much of the fighting. The few records that survive from that dark time provide only hints as to why that might have been, alluding to the existence of another, terrible war that took place beyond the sight of the wider Imperium, one that only the Adeptus Custodes had any chance of winning.

Still, the Ten Thousand did take part in two pivotal conflicts during the tumultuous years of the Heresy. These were the Razing of Prospero, arguably the first battle of that dreadful era, and the Siege of Terra.

The attack on Prospero came even before Horus tipped his hand in open rebellion. It was intended to be an act of censure, a punishment for the sorcerous Primarch Magnus the Red and his wayward Thousand Sons Legion. Upon their distant home world of Prospero the Thousand Sons had recklessly continued the use of psychic powers and empyric meddling in direct defiance of the Edict of Nikaea. None know for sure what finally forced the Emperor to intervene, but fragmentary sources tell of some psychic catastrophe on Terra, and an inescapable link to the powers of Magnus himself. Whatever the truth, Constantin Valdor and his Legio Custodes were charged with leading a force to Prospero

H eracal swept his guardian spear in a tight arc. Its powered blade sliced through ceramite, flesh and bone, sending the traitor's helm bouncing down the steps with the head still inside. Blood fountained, its colour rich red. Heracal raised one foot and kicked the swaying corpse in its midriff, sending it tumbling after its cranium. The Custodian scowled as two more traitors appeared at the bottom of the stairwell, clad in the panoply of the Sons of Horus. He levelled his guardian spear and let fly, directing a hail of bolt shells into the turncoats. One of them was blasted backwards, his chest-plate reduced to wreckage. The other weathered Heracal's fire and reciprocated, discharging his bolter even as he stormed up the steps.

Impacts rocked Heracal on his heels, but they couldn't pierce his auramite plate. A lesser warrior might have gloated, glorying in his supremacy. Instead, Heracal lunged forwards with lightning speed and drove his spear tip through the traitor's faceplate before he could dive aside.

'Clear here,' voxed Heracal, shaking the Space Marine's corpse disdainfully from his blade.

'West stair also clear,' came Lytanus' voice in response.

'Engaging at the northern arch,' voxed Artoris, and Heracal heard the sound of blades clashing and bolters roaring in the background. 'They're trying another push through the Peacemaker's Square.'

'That's three times now,' said Heracal, setting off at a jog towards the northern arch. 'Wiser men would have realised they cannot break us.'

'Wiser men would not have turned their backs upon the Emperor,' replied Lytanus.

'True,' said Heracal, hearing the sounds of gunfire swelling ahead. 'Then it falls to us to punish their foolishness.'

Rounding a corner, he cycled his guardian spear's autoloaders and ran through a mnemic assessment of the Peacemaker's Square, its approaches, fire arcs, blind spots and trap zones.

Another moment and he was at the northern arch, firelight and smoke spilling through it along with the din of battle. Heracal drew up shoulder to shoulder with Artoris, whose gold armour was drenched in the blood of the foe.

'Well met,' said Artoris, as he poured bolt shells into the traitor Space Marines charging through the burning gardens of the square.

'World Eaters,' spat Heracal, adding his fire to the salvo. 'Deranged savages.'

'Just so,' said Lytanus as he joined their impromptu firing line. 'Let us exterminate them.'

Together, the Custodians strode out to meet the World Eaters' charge. Every shot they fired was perfectly placed. Every step and blade swing was expertly timed, using the berserk traitors' momentum against them. As blood sprayed and Legiones Astartes corpses crashed to the ground, Heracal felt a stern determination and unflinching conviction within him. While a single Custodian yet lived, the Imperial Palace would never fall…

CONSTANTIN VALDOR

Few warriors in the entire history of the Imperium have even come close to the martial magnificence, selfless dedication and strategic excellence of Constantin Valdor, first Captain-General of the Ten Thousand. So exceptional a warrior was Valdor that it is said he could even have matched a Primarch in a contest of blades. Yet Valdor's value to the Emperor was so much more than as a mere combatant. From the earliest days of the Unification Wars – perhaps even before then – Constantin Valdor was the Emperor's staunch companion, and his loyalty to the Master of Mankind was absolute. The Captain-General would rather have taken his own life than risk that of the Emperor; Valdor's devotion to his master was such that there was no act he would not perform, no deed he would not consider, to ensure the Emperor's continued survival.

It is said that Constantin Valdor epitomised all that it means to be one of the Adeptus Custodes. Stoic, watchful, fiercely intelligent and – when required – a truly inspirational leader, Valdor was a true hero of the Imperium who never once faltered in his duty. It is not recorded what became of Valdor after the Emperor's withdrawal to the Golden Throne, but there are those who believe he serves the Emperor still…

'There are no bystanders in the war of life and death, no place the battle cannot reach; so fight it without remorse or relenting, for death will surely do the same.'

- Attributed to Captain-General Constantin Valdor

and bringing Magnus back to Terra to face his father's judgement. Since their earliest days the Custodians had always borne the Magisterium Lex Ultima, a mark of office that made them answerable only to the Emperor himself. Yet never before had they been charged with exercising its authority for such a daunting task. Still, Valdor did not shirk from his duty. What should have been a diplomatic coup became a murderous conflict when Leman Russ, the Primarch of the Space Wolves, joined his forces to Valdor's. Goaded by Horus' cunning words and driven by an instinctive dislike for his sorcerous brother, Russ took the role not of Magnus' captor, but his executioner. Though Valdor initially resisted Russ' urgings, his hand was forced when the corruption of the sorcerers of Prospero was revealed, and so he led his gold-armoured brethren to the surface of the damned world. Fighting alongside the Sisters of Silence, whose null powers warded off the Thousand Sons' psychic attacks, the Custodians slew many of Magnus' followers during that tragic battle. Only with the aid of Valdor's warriors were the Space Wolves able to extricate themselves from the slaughter before a howling warp rift consumed Prospero itself.

The aftermath of the events on Prospero was one of bewilderment and uncertainty. In comparison, by the time Horus' Traitor Legions brought their war to the throneworld, there was no doubt where the battle lines were drawn. During that titanic siege, the Legio Custodes fought alongside the loyalist Legions to defend the Emperor and his palace. They showed no mercy to the turncoat Space Marines. They did not waver, even as megatonnes of explosive death rained from the burning skies, even as daemonic abominations spilled through the veil of reality and renegade Titans hammered the palace walls with city-levelling weaponry. Valdor and his Ten Thousand fought valiantly during that nightmarish battle, driving back one offensive after another.

Despite their heroics, and to the eternal shame of the Legio Custodes, they failed in their ultimate duty. All through the Siege of Terra, Horus watched from his orbiting flagship, the *Vengeful Spirit*, coordinating the final battle from afar. Yet at the last, with Terra in flames and traitor forces rampaging through the palace's outer districts, Horus lowered the shields on his battle barge. Why he did this, none

can say. Perhaps some sliver of his old self remained, and sought to derail the Dark Gods' plans. Perhaps he simply wished to face the Emperor before the end, and to strike his father down by his own hand.

Whatever the case, the Emperor immediately gathered an elite force of Primarchs, Space Marines and Custodians, and led them in a teleport attack against Horus' unshielded ship. The battle that followed was horrific, the Emperor's force scattered throughout the tainted ship and forced to fight for their lives. Sanguinius, Primarch of the Blood Angels, fell to Horus' talon, but worse was to follow. Despite the best efforts of the Custodians, they could not overcome the unnatural might of Horus. Only the Emperor was able to defeat his rebellious gene-son, but the victory came at a terrible cost. Horus' powers shattered the Emperor's body, leaving him a ruined husk. The Master of Mankind would be consigned to the Golden Throne forever more, its sustaining technologies keeping him on the threshold of life. So enthroned, his immense psychic power continues to guide and protect the loyal people of the Imperium – should he ever perish, Mankind would surely follow soon after.

GUARDIANS OF THE GOLDEN THRONE

In the wake of the Horus Heresy, the Legio Custodes became the Adeptus Custodes. They donned mourning black, for theirs was a shame and a failing that they sought neither to forget nor be absolved of. Yet though they had met with defeat and tragedy, the Custodians' vigil did not falter for even a moment.

For ten thousand years the Adeptus Custodes have stood guard over the Golden Throne. In that time, not a single enemy has gained access to the Sanctum Imperialis.

The Custodians have many tasks upon Terra. It is they who watch over not just the great gates that lead to the Emperor's throne room, but all of the domains of the Imperial Palace. Considering the complex is a continent-sized sprawl of interconnected fortresses, cathedrums, armouries, dungeons, macro-habs, judiciariums, archives, sanctums, space ports and countless other structures, this is no mean feat.

It is the Adeptus Custodes alone who decide who will be permitted audience with the Emperor, and it is an honour that is granted only in the rarest of circumstances. They patrol the endless lines of petitioners that wend through the Imperial Palace, ever watchful for those of xenos taint or heretical bent who might have contrived to penetrate the structure's outer defences. They oversee

the soul-binding ritual that sees thousands of psykers each day drained of their life force in order to sustain the Emperor and his Astronomican.

The Adeptus Custodes guard the deepest vaults of the Imperial Palace, wherein lurk sanity-blasting secrets from the Dark Age of Technology. They despatch shield companies to inspect the defences of the Sol System, and to eliminate anything that presents even the slightest hint of a threat to the sanctity of Holy Terra. They play their endless Blood Games, one of their own number taking the role of invader or assassin to test their defences and, in doing so, to strengthen them still further.

For millennia the Custodians have gone about their duties, bound to traditions that have become ritual and rote. Yet even as the wider Imperium has stagnated around them, and the Emperor's servants have come to view them with a mixture of superstition and awe, the Adeptus Custodes have done what they can to fend off doubt and ennui, and have never permitted despair to take them. They barely notice the fleeting mortal men that scurry around their feet, and insist upon keeping even the most ardently loyal Space Marines at a spear's length, for what has proven fallible once may do so again. Yet this is a mantra the Custodians apply also to themselves, and thus they have never permitted themselves a moment of laxity or introspection. At times their Captain-General has stood amongst the High Lords of Terra. At others he has served as one of that council's most powerful advisors. Either way, the Adeptus Custodes continue to exercise the full authority of the Magisterium Lex Ultima, marshalling the defences of Terra as they see fit and answering to no one but their silent master in matters of security, sanctity and strength.

THE COMPANIONS

The Companions are a three-hundred-strong force that forms the direct bodyguard of the Emperor while he sits upon the Golden Throne. They are hand-picked for their duties by the Captain-General, who chooses his candidates based upon painstaking assessments of each warrior's performance in training and battle, as well as their mental acuity, spiritual fortitude and countless other indicative factors. There can be no more important duty in all of the Imperium than to shield the Emperor himself. As such, no consideration for rank or veteran status is given when appointing Custodians to the Companions, and those passed over in favour of younger or less experienced candidates take no offence.

The vigil of the Companions is unending, and though they are of course rotated out for brief periods of rest, it is still a purgatorial duty. Arrayed in ranks around the Golden Throne, these wardens stand for incredible lengths of time, unmoving, unspeaking, poised constantly upon the cusp of battle readiness in case the slightest threat were to present itself. It is mentally and spiritually exhausting, even for the demigods of the Adeptus Custodes, and so when the Captain-General judges that a Companion has served long enough they will be

rotated out with immediate effect, replaced by a fresh inductee to their ranks. Again, this is no mark of dishonour, merely a pragmatic admission that even a Custodian cannot perform such a taxing duty indefinitely. The longest any individual has stood the Companion's Watch was Astoran Kalos, who endured for a full century before at last surrendering his place amongst the silent ranks.

Those who have served amongst the Companions are more likely to lend their talents to the grim bodyguards known as the Aquilan Shields. Such Custodians have protected the lives of the greatest and most august personages in the Imperium, most notably the High Lords of Terra themselves. From the Master of the Navigators' Guild to the High Logisticar of the Adeptus Administratum, the Lord Militant of the Imperium to the shadowed Master of the Officio Assassinorum, former Companions have acted as guardians for them all. To the Ten Thousand such duties are simply an extension of their vows to protect the Emperor, in this case by safeguarding those assets most important to the successful running of his Imperium. Still, it is a role that has earned the Adeptus Custodes much favour in the eyes of Terra's noble elite.

SHADOWS AND ALCHEMY

It was the Emperor himself that invented the process by which the warriors of the Adeptus Custodes are created. More than ten thousand years later, the same processes are still utilised, remaining every bit as shrouded in secrecy and tradition as they were during the Great Crusade.

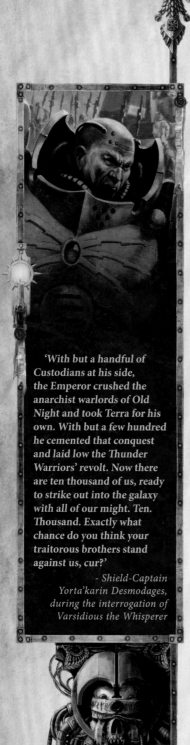

'With but a handful of Custodians at his side, the Emperor crushed the anarchist warlords of Old Night and took Terra for his own. With but a few hundred he cemented that conquest and laid low the Thunder Warriors' revolt. Now there are ten thousand of us, ready to strike out into the galaxy with all of our might. Ten. Thousand. Exactly what chance do you think your traitorous brothers stand against us, cur?'

- Shield-Captain Yorta'karin Desmodages, during the interrogation of Varsidious the Whisperer

If it can truly be said that the Space Marines are the sons of the Primarchs, then the Adeptus Custodes are the progeny of the Emperor himself. His might permeates them, his blessings so powerful that they can shield the Custodians from hurts both physical and empyric. The greatness of the Master of Mankind runs in their veins, burns in their eyes, and charges the air around them so that all faithful warriors instinctively respect and fear these demigods of war.

The method by which such remarkable individuals are created has always been known only to those of the Imperial household, and is carried out by the most accomplished chirurgeons and bio-alchemists of Terra within gilded laboratories locked away from the sight of Humanity's masses. With the Adeptus Custodes fighting only for the Emperor himself, and beholden to the commands and scrutiny of no other, the secrets of their recruitment have never been revealed, for not even the High Lords of Terra have the right to demand them.

It is known that all Custodians begin their lives as the infant sons of the noble houses of Terra. It is a mark of incredible prestige to surrender one's child to this most glorious of callings within the Imperium, and many notable clans amongst the Terran aristocracy have willingly given up almost entire generations of newborn sons to earn it.

Such children are taken in when they are still in infancy, for the earlier the genetic metamorphosis into a warrior of the Adeptus Custodes begins, the better a chance it has of success. Huge crowds line the Avenue of Sacrifice outside the Ascensor's Gate when such an intake occurs. They fill the air with frenzied cheering and prayer as the great and good of Terra's high society parade before them, soaking in the adoration of the masses even as they surrender their progeny forever into the Emperor's care.

There is a reason that – despite their remarkable lifespan – the Adeptus Custodes have never numbered more than approximately ten thousand warriors. Simply put, for every worthy aspirant who succeeds, thousands are found wanting. A Space Marine

is created by the introduction of gene-seed to the body, as well as the implantation of supporting organs. Between them, these modifications reshape those who receive them into living weapons. By comparison, whatever mysterious bio-alchemy is used to trigger the transformation into a Custodian occurs on an entirely deeper level, taking root in the cells, perhaps even the soul, of an aspirant.

The process of ascension goes beyond the purely physical and spiritual. Those who would join the brotherhood of the Adeptus Custodes are mentally indoctrinated; their psyches are rebuilt from the ground up, their mental architecture fortified as the Imperial Palace itself was fortified in the face of Horus' treachery, until it becomes an impregnable fastness or else collapses under its own weight.

Each aspirant endures thousands of hours of such psycho-indoctrination and mnemic conditioning. Their education is mercilessly absolute, information beaten into the metal of their minds at a punishing rate that drives many mad. They must grasp not only the tenets of warfare in all its forms, and learn every method of assassination, counter-espionage, threat recognition and death dealing known to Mankind, but also expand their minds in far more esoteric directions. Diplomacy and statecraft, astrogation and interstellar geography, history, philosophy, theosophy, artistry and countless other subjects must all be mastered to a breathtakingly high degree.

Much of this education is a throwback to the days when the Custodians were expected not only to provide the Emperor with protection, but also counsel and conversation. It has become a tradition applied by rote, but still its benefits are apparent. Not only does such an avalanche of information screen out those whose psyches are not sufficiently robust, but it further ensures that – almost alone in a dark and dreadful age – the Adeptus Custodes retain the enlightenment and perspective commonplace during the Great Crusade. Of course, with such blessings comes a tragic comprehension of the depths to which the Imperium has sunk; it is a credit to the Adeptus Custodes that such a realisation does not drive them to despair.

No truth is withheld from the Adeptus Custodes, for in order to do their duty without impediment they must possess all of the facts about the dark terrors that seek to conquer the galaxy. Such sanity-eroding revelations quickly eliminate those inductees who do not have sufficient spiritual fortitude to do their duty. Those that remain can be counted upon not only to understand the deeper ramifications of the war for the Emperor's realm, but to recognise why such truths must never be allowed to spread beyond their own ranks.

How long the process of creating a Custodian takes is unknown beyond the walls of the Imperial Palace. All those who survive emerge as magnificent praetorians, their sculpted physiques and altered minds so utterly other that they adopt entirely new personalities. They draw their names from ancient texts, deriving them from heroes, monsters and gods of old Terran mythology. Not only is this practice regarded as being entirely appropriate for such transcendent beings, it also allows the noble families of Terra to save face. All can – and will – claim that it was their offspring that showed the fortitude to become a Custodian, and none will gainsay them.

Though the minds of the Custodians are armoured against the machinations of witches and psykers, they themselves never exhibit such abilities. The Emperor allowed for no chink in the defences of his bodyguards, for while battlefield psykers are undoubtedly powerful living weapons, they are also unstable ones. Their minds are prone to invasion by warp entities, a danger that no member of the Adeptus Custodes need ever face.

For those superlative individuals that do survive to join the golden ranks, their comrades afford them immediate respect. There are no juniors amongst the Adeptus Custodes – only worthy warriors who understand the full burden of responsibility that their power and authority brings.

A Custodian's roll of honour is encompassed by his name. Though all begin with a single epithet, as these warriors achieve great deeds they are awarded additional names to reflect them. In days past, the Emperor himself would bestow these titles. Now it falls to the Captain-General, or occasionally a Shield-Captain in the field, to bestow the honour on his comrades. Custodians who have served for many centuries typically have dozens of names inscribed within the plates of their armour or – in some cases – even etched microscopically into their bones. Along with their name, ascension to the ranks of the Adeptus Custodes earns each individual their own armour and weapons. Entire bloodlines of exceptionally skilled artisans dwell within gilded towers on Terra, their purpose to fashion the auramite armour and perfectly balanced weapons for each new Custodian. Certain names such as the Clan Halbrinmir or the Clan Gestaxtis are renowned for their martial masterworks, and their augmetically enhanced artisan-barons are famed for the wonders they have wrought.

The Adeptus Custodes also have access to an incomparable armoury of technology, much of it dating back thousands of years. From the sleek Dawneagle jetbikes of the Vertus Praetors and the magnificent Allarus-pattern Terminator armour, to Land Raiders and Contemptor Dreadnoughts that saw battle during the Great Crusade, such equipment epitomises the proven excellence of all Adeptus Custodes materiel. The tools of war wielded by the Emperor's guardians never fail or falter, for they are handmade by the Imperium's most skilled smiths and maintained to the most painstaking standards imaginable. Just as the warriors who protect the Golden Throne must be utterly without fault or weakness, so must be the equipment they rely upon to discharge their duties.

These incredible armaments, the endless training regimes that the Custodians undergo, the years-long holo-conflicts through which they battle, and the shadow-shrouded wars they fight in the Emperor's name throughout the Sol System and far beyond – all these factors ensure that the Ten Thousand are the finest fighting force in the entire Imperium.

THE EYES OF THE EMPEROR

Though functionally immortal, even the warriors of the Adeptus Custodes eventually tire. Some suffer physical hurts that impact upon their ability to perform their duties, with lost limbs, artificial eyes or augmetic organs lessening their physical perfection. Others find their mental faculties beginning to erode, however slightly, acknowledging that their reaction times or mnemic awareness are not quite what they once were. For the vast majority of warriors, a tenth-of-a-second reduction in the speed at which blows are stuck or parried might be considered negligible. For a Custodian, it is error enough to necessitate that their watch come to an end.

When a Custodian judges himself no longer fit for duty he surrenders all of his equipment to the Hall of Armaments and vanishes into the void of the galaxy clad in hooded black robes. Such noble exiles still serve the Emperor, however, for wherever they travel they observe. Some work alone, dark and ominous figures slipping through the shadows of the Emperor's realm. Others cultivate networks of informants and agents, using fear and intimidation to secure compliance where loyalty and honour will not suffice.

Should they bear witness to a situation developing that they believe might threaten Terra or the Emperor, these watchers use secret channels to communicate a warning to the Captain-General. So do response forces of the Adeptus Custodes launch punitive and often pre-emptive strikes throughout the Imperium, forewarned of danger by the Eyes of the Emperor.

THE DEFENCES OF TERRA

The Emperor's palace on Terra is the largest and most impregnable defensive structure in the Imperium. It sprawls across an entire mountain range, stretching for thousands of miles over the surface of the throneworld. The Adeptus Custodes are responsible for the defence of this immense fortress, a duty they discharge with tireless diligence.

In the days of the Great Crusade, the Imperial Palace was a surpassing wonder of engineering. Yet the necessity to fortify that beautiful structure against the baleful intentions of Warmaster Horus – and the subsequent widespread devastation suffered at the hands of his traitor hordes – wrought irrevocable changes. In the wake of the heresy, the Imperial Palace was rebuilt as the mightiest fortress in human history. The ten millennia since have seen it become ever more bloated, polluted and immense. The palace's former asceticism lies buried beneath strata of gothic ornamentation and the brutal grandeur of the Cult Imperialis. What once was bright and magnificent is now vast and lowering, a hunched architectural monstrosity that wears its martial might like a challenge to the terrors of the darkling void. There can be no clearer metaphor for the fate of the wider Imperium, but though the palace is a grotesque mockery of its former self, still the Custodes guard it well.

This is no small task. The circumference of the palace's outermost walls is measured in thousands of miles. The towering spires

of its macro-habs and space ports break through the atmosphere and rise into the void like the spines of some bioluminescent beast. Its sub-levels dig deep into Terra's holy bedrock, in some places reaching a depth of hundreds of miles below the surface. Its corridors, chambers, vaults, fastnesses and plazas are so multitudinous that no single record remains to list them all, and the societal sub-nations, clan holdings and techno-urbanic serf tribes that dwell within its walls could populate entire star systems.

Despite this, the Adeptus Custodes have always proven equal to the duty of overseeing the palace's defence. It is they who patrol the colossal and seemingly endless walls, who stand guard over the sanctums and armouries, who patrol the petitioners' highways, the famed space ports and the vast fortifications. They inspect the endless miles of orbital guns and defensive silos, and maintain a wary guard over the hidden vaults deep within the palace which contain secrets so dreadful that they could bring about the fall of Humanity were they ever released.

And yet, the Adeptus Custodes find the manpower and dedication to do so much more. For thousands of years, their shield hosts have mustered in secret and set out aboard requisitioned warships to strike down threats identified by the roaming Eyes of the Emperor. Bands of Custodians have regularly patrolled the Sol System, serving as rotating garrisons for military facilities based around Luna, Venus, Pluto and numerous deep-space star fortresses that watch the approaches to Terra.

The Adeptus Custodes have also long liaised with the Imperial Fists Space Marine Chapter, who still maintain their role as joint guardians of the Sol System, and whose immense star fort – known as *Phalanx* – has often held a protective orbit over the throneworld.

The Adeptus Custodes have remained unwavering in these duties for thousands of years. Now, even as the galaxy darkens around them and new wars arise for them to fight, they are more determined than ever to ensure the Imperial Palace, and the whole of Terra, stand inviolable.

THE IMPERIAL PALACE

Being a cartographic representation of the most holy demesnes of the Imperial Palace on Terra

THE TOWER AQUILANE

THE INDOMITOR BASTION

THE DARK CELLS

THE NEXUS ADMINISTRATA

THE SANCTUM OF A THOUSAND EYES

THE SANCTUM IMPERIALIS

THE LION'S GATE

ASCENSOR'S GATE

AVENUE OF SACRIFICE

THE SPRAWL MAGNIFICAN

FORTRESS OF THE TRIBUNATE

VIGILATUM ORBITAL BATTERY

KATABATIC SLOPES

THE VICTORIS ABSOLUTE

The immensity of the Imperial Palace is breathtaking in its magnificence. Towering even taller than the mountain range upon which it was built, it is a monument to the grandiose martial might of Humanity.

'A wise man draws his swords when the time is right to wield them. A fool dies with blades still sheathed, fearing that there might yet come a time of greater need. For the sake of Emperor and Imperium both, we must take the fight to our enemies.'

- *Trajann Valoris to Roboute Guilliman in the wake of the Lion's Gate Incursion*

RISE OF THE PRIMARCH

In the last days before the gathering storm broke and the Great Rift tore the void in two, a bright light of hope was kindled within the galactic empire of Ultramar. Through great sacrifice and unnatural artifice, Roboute Guilliman, Primarch of the Ultramarines, was restored from the brink of death. His coming would herald great changes for the Imperium.

When the Traitor Legions fell upon the Imperial Palace at the culmination of the Horus Heresy, Roboute Guilliman and his Ultramarines were too far away to fight in their father's defence. Perhaps, had it been otherwise, the fate of the galaxy would have been very different.

Whatever the case, following his revival Guilliman was determined that he would not make the same mistake twice. Seeing the darkness rising to swamp the Imperium, he launched a desperate crusade across the stars that brought him by strange and bloody roads to the throneworld itself.

Guilliman was welcomed with all honour on Terra, permitted audience with the Emperor by Aquila Commander Kalim Varanor and reinstated as Lord Commander of the Imperium by an assemblage of the High Lords of Terra. Though the returned Primarch remained outwardly stern and regal, he had been shaken to the core by what had become of his father's empire. He quickly began instating changes that would permit the Imperium to fight back against the onrushing hordes of Chaos, bulldozing the bureaucratic stubbornness and hidebound pedantry of the Adeptus Terra as he went.

Guilliman's return came not a moment too soon, for he had not been long at his labours when the cascading fury of the Great Rift washed over the Sol System. Though not directly struck by warp storms, Terra bore the brunt of empyric shock waves that temporarily extinguished the light of the Astronomican, and wrought havoc and misery from the planet's highest spires to its deepest crypts. The Adeptus Custodes found themselves putting down riots, doomsday cult uprisings and rampaging packs of luckless petitioners driven to madness and cannibalism. Bands of Custodian Wardens stood their ground in the shadowed undervaults far beneath the palace as runic sigils burned out and timeless horrors burst from their containment cells.

Worse was to follow. Seeking to strike the decapitating blow that would bring the Imperium to ruin, a vast horde of Khornate

Daemons tore through the skin of reality and assaulted the Lion's Gate. Legions of howling Daemons surged towards the Emperor's palace in a crimson tidal wave, and a frenzied battle ensued.

The battleship-sized gun emplacements flanking the Lion's Gate blasted glowing craters in the diabolical horde, but alone they had no hope of prevailing. Led by Roboute Guilliman and Captain-General Valoris, a combined host of the Adeptus Custodes, Ultramarines and Sisters of Silence marched out to meet the Daemons before the walls of the Emperor's palace.

In scenes that echoed the horror of the Siege of Terra ten millennia before, the golden warriors of the Adeptus Custodes faced the Blood God's savage butchers blade to blade. This time, led by some of the Imperium's greatest champions and driven by a furious determination never to fail again, they prevailed. One by one, the eight Bloodthirsters that led the attack were blown apart or cut down. The cost in lives was great, with noble defenders who had stood guard over the Emperor for thousands of years brought low by the brazen weapons of Khorne's hateful Daemons. Yet even as the skies boiled blood-red and carmine rains slicked the ground, the legions of Khorne faded from reality with howls of frustration and rage.

The Lion's Gate Incursion proved a stark truth. While great swathes of witnesses were corralled and exterminated by the Inquisition, and efforts made to obliterate

all evidence of the conflict, the masters of the Adeptus Custodes formally recognised that Terra's defence could no longer be guaranteed without greater proactive measures. If the servants of the Dark Gods had bypassed the defences of the cradle of Humanity.

Behind locked doors, complex wards and layers of psy-protections, Valoris and Guilliman ratified a formal amendment to the role of the Adeptus Custodes. The palace must still be guarded, of course, and the Companions' watch must continue within the Emperor's throne room. However, as a logical extension of the vows of duty they had sworn, the Adeptus Custodes committed to greatly extending their extra-solar activities.

Aided by oracular doomscryers and alpha-level astropathic intercepts, and guided in part by the continued efforts of the Eyes of the Emperor, more shield hosts than ever before struck out from Terra. The aim of these forces was to exterminate utterly the most deadly threats to the Emperor himself. This mission might take them all across the galaxy, even into the shadows of the Imperium Nihilus beyond the sprawl of the Great Rift, but always their focus would be the sanctity of Terra. In this capacity a number of shield companies attached themselves to Guilliman's Indomitus Crusade, reprising the role of the Emperor's emissaries in bearing Primaris reinforcements and technology to the beleaguered Space Marine Chapters, and ensuring they understood that this was a gift from the Master of Mankind himself. It was not to be squandered or refused.

Other shield companies relocated to permanently garrison the Sol System's outer defences, or travelled further afield in order to watch over the primary warp routes that remained stable paths to the throneworld. Others still took even more esoteric mantles, becoming hunters after arch-heretics, questors for artefacts crucial to the ongoing survival of the Imperium, or redoubling their efforts in their wars against Humanity's hidden foes. Not since the Great Crusade had so many Custodians bestrode the stars…

A HOST OF HEROES

From outside, the organisation of the Ten Thousand seems byzantine. When they deign to account themselves at all to other Imperial bodies their ranks appear complex and highly stratified. Yet much of this is tradition, or else purposeful misdirection; in practice, the Adeptus Custodes use a robust and easily adaptable system to organise their forces.

The Adeptus Custodes operate as a military force, a gathering of champions each of whom possesses unassailable authority over virtually any other organisation in the Imperium. Conversely, no Imperial agent can give a Custodian orders. Even such worthies as the High Lords of Terra and Lord Commander Guilliman are able only to request – not demand – their aid.

As befits such a body of elite warriors, the internal hierarchy of the Adeptus Custodes is remarkably flat. The Captain-General commands the Ten Thousand, inheriting a post that has been passed down from one gallant leader to the next ever since the mysterious disappearance of Constantin Valdor. The Captain-General has absolute authority over the Custodes, acting as the ritual proxy for the Emperor himself and speaking with the voice of the Master of Mankind.

Beneath the Captain-General is the Custodian Tribunate, a group of ten veteran Custodians who act as advisors to the Captain-General. Membership of this body changes periodically to ensure a blend of established wisdom and fresh ideas. A Custodian must have earned at least ten names before he can serve on the Tribunate, and have led his comrades

victoriously in battle on at least three occasions. Once he joins the Tribunate, a Custodian must serve for at least ten years. During this time he will not see the front lines, for he is too busy bending all of his considerable intellect to supporting – strategically and diplomatically – the Captain-General.

Below this ruling council are the Shield-Captains, who fulfil the roles of inspiring leaders, gifted generals and selfless champions. Their titles vary enormously, from Supreme Castellans and Aquila Commanders to Master Guardians, often borne in accordance with the specific duties to which they have been assigned. It is Shield-Captains that take charge of the Adeptus Custodes' military engagements; one is typically afforded overall command of an operation, while several others of his rank may lend him their strength and wisdom in a supporting capacity.

The remainder of the Custodians possess roughly equivalent status to one another, forming loose warrior bands traditionally known as sodalities. There are varying strategic roles within the organisation to which some Custodians find themselves better suited. However, whether this be the rapid jetbike troops of the Vertus Praetors,

the heavy assault specialists of the Allarus Custodians, or the unwavering Wardens, they still operate within a meritocracy that sees them afforded whatever honour their comrades believe them worthy of.

A singular force of the Adeptus Custodes is referred to as a shield company. The numbers within such a formation can vary considerably, hand-picked by their Shield-Captain for the task at hand and ranging from a small band to a sizeable army complete with jetbikes, tanks and Dreadnoughts. Under normal circumstances, a shield company includes no more than one Shield-Captain and perhaps thirty to forty Custodians.

When a larger force is required, multiple shield companies gather into forces known as shield hosts. Led by conclaves of Shield-Captains and boasting tens, sometimes hundreds of Custodians, shield hosts have the martial strength to crush enemy armies and bring entire star systems to heel. The gathering of such might is a momentous undertaking – a shield host is only assembled to accomplish those tasks that no other Imperial force could be trusted with, and its warriors march to war with a singular and implacable determination to enact the Emperor's will.

THE MISERICORDIA

When an aspirant ascends to the ranks of the Adeptus Custodes, he is presented with a beautifully fashioned knife known as a misericordia. These weapons are filigreed with gold and theldrite, their hilts moulded to the owner's unique grip and their blades imbued with micromolecular dissonator spirits that allow them to slice through the thickest armour as though it wasn't there at all.

More than a lethal sidearm, the misericordia signifies something greater. Its traditional meaning is said to date all the way back to the darkest days of Terran history, when cruel warlords ruled by the blade alone. These weapons of oppression were known as misericordia. Yet as the Emperor led his wars of unification, his Custodians are believed to have co-opted the term for their own use. No longer would the misericordia be a symbol of tyrannical rule. Instead, it came to represent the right of the bearer to act as the arbiter of the Emperor's judgement, and to put to death those tyrants, lunatics and demagogues who stood against him.

The misericordia still shows its wielder to be the Emperor's sanctioned executioner, yet since his fall these blades bear a second, grimmer meaning. They have become weapons of vengeance, to be turned upon those who betrayed the Emperor and left him a broken shell. Every time a misericordia is plunged into a traitor's heart, so it is said, a minuscule measure of revenge is exacted on behalf of the Emperor himself. Though the Custodians are typically immune to such superstition, there are those amongst their ranks who harbour the hope that if enough traitor blood is spilt with these blades, it may in some way restore their master. Another school of thought, the adherents of which are known as the Miserians, believe that through the wounds inflicted with misericordia they will slowly bleed the great descendants of Horus, inflicting a death by a thousand cuts upon the Black Legion and their masters. Thus, though Custodians have the right to carry their misericordia or not as they see fit, it is rare indeed that they go to battle against the Heretic Astartes without these blades at their hips.

CUSTODES DEPLOYMENTS

The Adeptus Custodes differ from the vast majority of Imperial military organisations in that their armies obey only the loosest regimentation. Those Custodians that lead each force are permitted vast autonomy in selecting whatever forces they believe they will require to complete their mission, with only the broadest organisational guidelines by which to abide.

THE GILDED TALONS SHIELD COMPANY

SHIELD-CAPTAIN

Typically, a shield company is led by a single Shield-Captain, though sometimes it will include additional champions who act as his companions.

CUSTODIAN GUARD	CUSTODIAN GUARD	VEXILUS PRAETOR	ALLARUS TERMINATORS	VERTUS PRAETORS

The Gilded Talons shield company fights under the leadership of Shield-Captain Archturus Paliades. As is typical with such organisations, their members often fight amongst the ranks of other shield companies also, but when Paliades calls, all of his comrades who can will answer. The composition of this shield company was determined by the Shield-Captain to suit his strategic needs; others might contain wildly different arrays of troop types and vehicles.

Imperatus Auxila
- Land Raider *Glorious Wrath*
- Land Raider *Justice Delivered*
- Contemptor, Talorian
- Contemptor, Euramedes
- Seconded Cruiser *Voidhawk*
- Phemus, Eye of the Emperor

Supporting assets attached to shield companies are designated as Imperatus Auxila. These range from war engines and Dreadnoughts to seconded warships, and even non-combatant field agents.

THE SOLAR FURIES SHIELD HOST

COMMANDERS

A shield host is typically commanded by multiple Shield-Captains, supported by the wise counsel of several Vexilus Praetors.

SHIELD COMPANY	SHIELD COMPANY	SHIELD COMPANY	SHIELD COMPANY	SHIELD COMPANY

The Solar Furies first assembled in late M36, to battle against a Necron awakening on a world perilously close to Terra. They have fought together many times since, typically gathering to eliminate suddenly arising threats close to or within the Sol System. It is important to note that the Solar Furies is a very large shield host – any formation that brings two or more shield companies together beneath the leadership of multiple Shield-Captains is considered to be a shield host.

Maximus Auxila
- 10 Venerable Land Raiders
- 7 Contemptor Dreadnoughts
- Adeptus Custodes Falchion-class battleship, the *Starfire*
- 5 co-opted Imperial warships
- Various field agents

Shield hosts gather all the auxiliary assets of their shield companies under the single umbrella heading of Maximus Auxila. From a practical point of view, however, these assets still fight with their parent shield companies.

UNIFORMS AND HERALDRY

Each Custodian's armour and weapons are crafted specifically for them by hand. Thus, each suit of armour is an individual work of exceptional craftsmanship with its own unique flourishes and decorations. Yet all Custodians maintain certain standardised elements to their wargear that help them to quickly identify one another's place both on and off the battlefield.

1. The right shoulder guard of a Custodian's armour depicts the Imperial Aquila, a sigil of eternal vigilance and a sign of the Custodian's mandate to enact – by force if necessary – the will of the Emperor himself.

2. The gems set into each Custodian's armour are individually mined from deep beneath the surface of Terra and hand cut by skilled artisans. Their colouration is flawlessly precise, an art form in its own right, not only across the Custodian's armour, but across that of his entire shield company. When a Custodian switches from one such organisation to another, the stones will be carefully extracted from his armour and replaced with those of an appropriate colour if needs be.

3. The colour panels on the Custodian's left shoulder guard show clearly to which shield company or shield host they belong. The latter organisational tier takes precedence for these purposes. This colouration will often match the Custodian's tabard, along with any robes he may wear.

4. All Adeptus Custodes armour is made from the incredibly rare substance known as auramite. Its natural colouration is a lustrous gold, a hue entirely appropriate for the Emperor's personal guardians. However, through closely guarded alchemical processes, auramite can be tinted, or its colour changed altogether on a molecular level. It is a painstaking and costly process, but considered far more suited to the Custodians' importance than simple repainting.

5. The haft or hilt of a Custodian's weapon is sometimes worked – or, in many cases, reworked – to match the colouration of their armour. This is not standard amongst all shield companies, however.

THE SHADOWKEEPERS

WARDERS OF THE DARK CELLS

There are terrible things locked away beneath the Emperor's palace, eldritch terrors from the depths of Old Night that could annihilate the Imperium. To the Shadowkeepers falls the duty of standing guard over them unto the end of time.

The Shadowkeepers hold the keys to the rune-locked portals hidden deep beneath the Imperial Palace. They alone know the ways by which the runic locks may be disengaged, the wards unbound and the sanctic circles breached. They alone know that these things must never happen, for the Dark Cells hold such horrors at bay that Mankind's sanity would not survive their release. A full shield host is devoted to this grim responsibility, over a hundred Custodians patrolling the dark and silent corridors, vigilantly watching over the last terrors of Old Night. It is a task that would soon drive most men mad, for though neither sight nor sound can escape the forbidden cells, the air of those corridors is charged with dread. A perpetual menace thickens the shadows and makes them crawl. Even the superhumans of the Adeptus Custodes are forever on edge in those dark oubliettes, for the sense of unspeakable threat never wanes. It is a testament to the discipline and spiritual fortitude of the Shadowkeepers that they stand their guard unflinching, sometimes for decades at a time.

The ranks of this shield host include many Custodian Wardens, whose oaths of protection help them to focus upon the task at hand to the exclusion of all else. The leaders of these forbidding sentries carry ancient weapons of mysterious provenance, their use intended as a last resort should anything ever break free from the Dark Cells.

For ten thousand years the Shadowkeepers have performed their duty, yet the coming of the Great Rift changed everything. With the power of Chaos spilling raw and seething into the spaces between the stars, new abominations have come to light. Worse still are the cells that stand suddenly empty, the entities and artefacts once contained within spirited away by some unholy force to curse the galaxy once more. Fearing the consequences of such dread remnants of the Age of Strife falling into the wrong hands, the Shadowkeepers at last sent warriors out into the galaxy. These jailers must trammel that which should not be, slaughtering all who seek to impede them, before returning their foul prizes to the cells where they belong.

THE LOCKWARDEN

There have been many Shield-Captains charged with mastery of the Shadowkeepers. This appointment confers the title of Lockwarden, a name that is borne in perpetuity and garners solemn respect from every other member of the Ten Thousand. The Lockwarden must be the sternest of all guardians, the most unrelenting and alert gaoler on the face of Terra. Moreover, should any creature or relic escape the Dark Cells, or newly emerged threat need to be imprisoned therein, it is the duty of the Lockwarden to personally oversee the operation.

The current incumbent of this position is Shield-Captain Borsa Thursk, who has been Lockwarden for a century and a half. He is a grim and frighteningly intense warrior whose utter fearlessness and steely vigilance make him ideal for his role. It speaks volumes about the dire condition of the galaxy that Thursk left Terra but twice before the breaking of the storm, yet he has barely set foot there since the Great Rift yawned wide.

Custodian Warden Jaeharl Feldorus Ghau, who stands amongst the steely eyed ranks of the Shadowkeepers. The sable of Ghau's armour is one with the gloom of the Dark Cells, while the rich crimson of his left shoulder guard and robes complete the attire of his shield host. Custodian Ghau has guarded the Dark Cells for seventeen years, during which time he has been called upon to leave Terra thrice on heavily veiled reclamation missions. It was Ghau's blade that slew the Slithering Dreamer on Tarnus IV, a grim achievement that is reflected in the new names inscribed within his black armour.

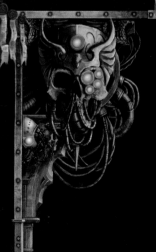

THE AQUILAN SHIELD
THE GILDED GUARDIANS

Certain servants of the Emperor bear great responsibilities deemed directly relevant to the safety of Terra. Such esteemed figures are afforded the protection of the Aquilan Shield, at least until their usefulness is thought to be at its end.

As the doomscryers of the Imperial Palace sift the tides of the empyrean for warnings of disaster, they also take note of those who – through example, thought or deed – are likely to avert such catastrophes before they threaten the Golden Throne. These fated individuals are honoured with the protection of the Aquilan Shield, for in this way a small band of Custodians can ensure a significant martial or spiritual asset survives to act in the Emperor's defence.

The Aquilan Shield are an informal brotherhood laced through the ranks of the Adeptus Custodes. They typically operate in small warrior bands, journeying across the stars to stand watch over their charges wherever they may be. No warning is given nor permission asked – the warriors of the Aquilan Shield appear as if from nowhere, avatars of the Emperor's will who announce their quarry to be under the protection of the Master of Mankind. Such an honour is beyond compare, and is never refused no matter the circumstances or the individual chosen.

The Aquilan Shield have acted as bodyguards to High Lords, Sororitas Canonesses, Lord Inquisitors, Astra Militarum generals and Space Marine Captains. They have even protected two crusade leaders bearing the title of Warmaster, staunchly ignoring the historic associations with he who first held that rank. Yet they have also appeared amidst flares of golden light to watch over firebrand front-line preachers, bewildered militia leaders and others of apparently little import. The only unifying factor amongst them all is that, while attending their duties beneath the gimlet gaze of the Emperor's own guards, these individuals are expected to achieve incredible things in the defence of the throneworld. The Aquilan Shield fight to ensure such a future comes to pass, shielding their charges from harm until the exact moment the usefulness of the person under their protection is deemed spent. At that point they depart without a word, leaving those they guarded to look to their own defence. Tragedy often follows, but this is of no concern to the Aquilan Shield – providing it does not jeopardise the safety of the Golden Throne.

'The duty of the Emperor's defence does not end at the walls of the Imperial Palace. Our war is like an endless game of regicide, played over countless boards against infinite foes at once. In such a contest one must be constantly pre-emptive, always cunning and ever ready to seize any advantage that presents itself. Our gaze must rove far afield, and our every move must be perfectly executed. To do any less is to court final defeat.'

- Captain-General
Trajann Valoris

Tauramacchis Ossian is a Custodian Warden who has stood amongst the ranks of the Aquilan Shield for over four centuries. His allegiance is indicated by the royal purple colouration of his left shoulder guard and his robes. In his time amongst the Aquilan Shield, Ossian has defended the life of Arch-Cardinal Mumbres from daemonic assassins, watched over High Lord Veynd during the Red Razor Uprisings, and protected a bewildered young preacher named Lorrin from the horrors of the war on Phinalium until the priest's selfless martyrdom earned him sainthood and turned the tide of a war across an entire sector.

THE DREAD HOST
INSTRUMENT OF THE EMPEROR'S WRATH

Fear is a familiar weapon to the Imperium, used to deter enemies and keep seething populations in line. Yet there is no terror as pure and absolute as that invoked when the Emperor's own fury is unleashed to punish his foes.

The Dread Host represents a breathtaking concentration of military might. It numbers hundreds of Custodians, organised into multiple shield hosts and transported aboard a trio of pre-heresy warships known as the *Moiraides*. The nature of this army is simple: they are the deliverers of the Emperor's judgement, his anger and his punishment made manifest.

Not for them the pinpoint rapid strike, the hidden war or the measured defensive action. Instead, the assembled Shield-Captains of the Dread Host identify the most visible and dramatic threats to the Segmentum Solar and unleash upon them such overwhelming annihilation that it sends shock waves rolling through the warp itself. Sometimes one warship is sent, sometimes two; only a handful of times in the entire history of the Imperium have all three of the *Moiraides* loosed their passengers against a single foe. Yet always the effect is the same. Spearheaded by dozens of Allarus Custodians, the Dread Host fall upon their victims with unstoppable

force. They slaughter the enemy's warriors and reduce their war engines to wreckage. They cast down their false idols and set them aflame. They topple their cities, sunder their strongholds, and butcher their allies and followers. They make grisly examples of those who would dare lead such a challenge to the Emperor's dominion, ignoring all attempts at surrender and foiling all bids at flight. By the time the Dread Host are done with their war, nothing remains of their chosen victims but the gruesome tales of their brutal demise at the Emperor's hand.

The Dread Host have smashed Ork Waaaghs!, obliterated rebellious star systems and crushed traitor crusades. They have fought against enemies thousands of times their number and humbled them through strategy, speed and strength. With every campaign they spread the terror of the Emperor's wrath.

The breathtaking bloodshed and absolute destruction they leave in their wake has dissuaded hundreds of uprisings and invasions before they could even begin.

Custodian Guard Kallisarian Tristraen Desh has been a member of the Dread Host for only six months. In that time, he has already taken part in two separate military campaigns within a galactic stone's throw of Terra. During the purge on Chormium, he ruthlessly slew well over two hundred renegade guardsmen. At the battle for the corvinium mines of Triton, Desh impaled a Genestealer Patriarch, ending its perilous cult uprising in a sizzling spray of ichor. He proudly displays the sable shoulder guard and white pteruges of his shield host, which is itself one of several that currently wear the colours of the Dread Host.

THE SANCTUM OF A THOUSAND EYES

The stronghold of the Dread Host rises to dominate an entire district of the Imperial Palace. This armoured bastion is lit with electro-braziers and arc-lumen of immense size, all angled to under-light the five hundred enormous eagle statues that line the Sanctum's upper battlements. Each as large as a super-heavy tank, these ominous sculptures are posed in vigilant stances, many staring up into the stellar gulf while the remainder peer down upon the thronging processionals below. Superstition runs rife that the eagles of the Sanctum of a Thousand Eyes can perceive disloyalty no matter where it lies, and that the Emperor looks through their avian eyes to see the darkness in men's hearts. To some extent this is true; each eagle contains a complex array of long-range augurs, servitor cogitation banks and multi-spectral listening devices that feed floods of information down into the Sanctum's data-shrines. This information is used by the Dread Host to isolate and annihilate threats to the Golden Throne.

THE SOLAR WATCH

CASTELLANS OF THE BLESSED WORLDS

The Sol System is amongst the most heavily fortified of Mankind's stellar holdings. The Adeptus Custodes consider its worlds, star forts and space lanes to be extensions of their master's palace, and ensure they are guarded accordingly.

From the vast orbital fortresses of Luna to the cloud-keeps of Jupiter and the deep-space star forts of the Halo Belt, Humanity maintains hundreds of strongholds throughout the Sol System. Billions of weapons point menacingly into the dark gulfs of space, ready to unleash spectacular devastation upon any foolish enough to threaten Mankind's seat of power. Armoured towers and gargoyle-festooned bastions loom over every approach, sanctified against the foul machinations of the Emperor's many foes. Entire fleets of Imperial Navy ships prowl the space lanes, vigilant for the slightest threat. Yet perhaps the most formidable of all Terra's outer defensive measures are the Custodians of the Solar Watch.

Consisting of several shield companies of varying strength, the Solar Watch swear binding oaths to keep guard over the outer bastions of the throneworld. They see themselves as the first true line of defence for the Imperial Palace, and believe that it is their duty to ensure that no external threat ever makes it as far as Terra. To this end,

they constantly patrol routes between the worlds and void structures of the Sol System, ever vigilant for danger.

Though they typically travel via naval craft and intrastellar trade ships, the Solar Watch maintain a formidable concentration of Venerable Land Raiders, and are typically able to deploy forces that are predominately, if not entirely, mechanised. This allows them to respond swiftly, and with overwhelming force, to any potentially threatening situation that may develop. While such dangers are not common within the Sol System, they are certainly not unheard of; the Solar Watch have been instrumental in bringing an end to Daemon-worshipping cults, Inquisitorial coups and subtle xenos incursions on every world bar Mars. While their authority technically extends to the red planet, the Adeptus Custodes are wise enough to maintain cordial relations with the servants of the Omnissiah, and so travel to that world only occasionally, trusting the Cult Mechanicus to police its own deviants.

TALON SORTIES

The more aggressive of the Captain-Generals have traditionally charged the Solar Watch with performing sporadic Talon Sorties. These involve the watch gathering shield-company-strength forces and launching strikes against prevailing threats in the systems closest to Terra.

The Solar Watch do not waste their resources in war zones already heavily invested in by Imperial forces. Rather, they sally out to destroy developing threats or eliminate enemies that have broken existing Imperial lines. Deploying aboard their Venerable Land Raiders, they slam into their enemies in fast-moving armoured spearheads. Prioritising the slaughter of command elements and heavy combat assets, the Solar Watch cripple their enemies' capacity to function as an army of conquest before abruptly withdrawing, leaving lesser Imperial forces to mop up what remains. After all, the duty of guarding the Sol System is a vital one, and the Solar Watch cannot leave their posts for long.

Pydanoris Calligus fights as part of the Solar Watch. He is the eldest and most respected warrior within his squad, always lending his steady and uncompromising counsel to his comrades and ensuring that no detail is missed, no advantage conceded and no foe given even a moment's respite. Clad in the marble-white and red of the Solar Watch, Calligus and his squad have boarded mass-conveyor barges that turned out to be packed with cultists, decimated the garrisons of defence platforms found negligent in their duties, and sallied out under Shield-Captain Thetus to cut the head from a cabal of xenos flesh-witches on Yorlos before they could work their evils against the Golden Throne.

EMISSARIES IMPERATUS
HERALDS OF THE GOLDEN THRONE

In the days of the Great Crusade, the Emperor often entrusted crucial messages or artefacts to be borne by his Custodians. It is a duty they still fulfil now, speaking with the authority of the Master of Mankind himself.

Though the Emperor has long been confined to the Golden Throne, there are those amongst the Ten Thousand who claim to hear their master's voice during their meditations, and to feel his hand guiding them. To their comrades there is no implication of divine intervention in this, for the Custodes have never viewed the Emperor as a god. They merely see their liege's indomitable will at work, reaching out from his shattered frame to direct his praetorians as he did when he could still walk amongst them.

Those who feel the Emperor's guidance the keenest become Emissaries Imperatus. They band together in like-minded groups and, through discussion and meditation, interpret what it is that the Master of Mankind wishes them to do. With the tacit approval of the Captain-General, they bear the Emperor's words across the Imperium to commanders who must hear them, or occasionally unlock some ancient device from the palace vaults and bequeath it to whichever champion can wield it best. Their words have redirected entire crusades, and seen threats intercepted and archeotech riches won that might otherwise have passed the Emperor's servants by.

For thousands of years the Emissaries Imperatus have been seen abroad, but rarely and in small numbers. Yet with the return of Guilliman and the commencement of the Indomitus Crusade, their activity has increased considerably. When the Primarch announced his intention to bear the secrets of the Primaris Space Marines to the loyalist Chapters, there was some resistance from the Adeptus Custodes, who feared strengthening those who might one day rebel against the Emperor once again. Yet dozens of Emissaries Imperatus stepped forwards to intercede, stating this was the will of the Emperor. They accompanied Guilliman's Crusade, many of them taking to the air as Vertus Praetors, the quicker to deliver messages of reinforcement to the embattled Space Marines. The presence of the Adeptus Custodes also ensured that even the most traditional Chapters accepted the Primaris warriors into their ranks. One does not decline a gift from the Emperor's own hand, after all.

'Through the artifice of the Martian priesthood were these warriors created. By the grace of the almighty Emperor are they given now to you. Silence your questions and instead rejoice at the honour done to you this day. You are handed the gift of hope by the immortal Master of Mankind himself, and you will accept it with sincere and solemn gratitude lest you be taken for the traitors that you profess to hate.'

- Sanash Gallimedan, Emissary Imperatus to the Hammers of Dorn Chapter

Archimallus Tychor has been an Emissary Imperatus for over one thousand years. He fights as part of the Custodian Warden squad known as the Veritas Proclamation, proudly wearing the red shoulder guard and grey-white robes of his shield company. It was Tychor's Emperor-given insights that guided Adeptus Mechanicus Explorator Crusade Gamma-Hades to the archeotech treasures of Heng's World. It was his blade, too, that slew dozens of the massive Orks who had already claimed that world's techno-riches for their own. The Veritas Proclamation had only just returned to Terra when the Great Rift opened, and they were among the first to speak out in favour of the Indomitus Crusade.

THE SOLAR FASTNESS

There was a time when the wholesale invasion of Terra was utterly unthinkable. With the opening of the Great Rift, that time has passed. The Sol System today boasts some of the most formidable fortifications in the galaxy, manned by determined warriors and shielded by technology and faith. Yet still the greatest lynchpin of its defence is the Adeptus Custodes.

Were some courageous or foolhardy invader to approach the Sol System, they would find themselves assailed before they had even cleared the Mandeville point – that region of a system's outer boundaries beyond which it is safe to translate from warp space to the real. The system's halo-belt plays host to massive star forts, garrisoned by dedicated regiments of Astra Militarum and empyrically tethered in place. The rest of the outer system is densely laced with thousand-mile-wide fields of void mines, prowling system monitors and huge, vacuum-hardened hunter servitors of terrifying aspect.

Were the invader to overcome these hazards, they would find resistance stiffening the deeper they pushed into the system. Heavy naval patrols from the Battlefleet Solar thunder through the darkness, their craggy silhouettes presaging death to any who fall beneath their sights. Monitor-shrines, dock-fortresses, fighter bases and countless weapons platforms dot the darkness, their lumen winking like artificial constellations. The Grey Knights, the Inquisition and the Adeptus Mechanicus all have holdings within the Sol System, boasting suitably ferocious defences. Moreover, since Guilliman's Throneworld Decree, Terra and her sister worlds can raise greater forces in their own defence than ever before.

When coupled with the efforts of the Solar Watch, and the presence of the Imperial Fists' mighty battle station *Phalanx* hanging in geostationary orbit above Terra, it is clear that the defences of the Sol System are all but impenetrable to invading armies. Yet there are subtler threats to the Golden Throne, and it is against these that the Adeptus Custodes must be especially vigilant.

From all across the Imperium come endless streams of pilgrims, merchants, bureaucrats, adepts, zealots, emissaries, refugees and countless others. Thousands of ships translate from the warp every day, entering strictly coordinated approach corridors that lead them to Venus, Mars, Jupiter, Luna and Terra itself. Every world and moon in the Sol System – barring a few mysterious exceptions – is ringed with habitats and docking platforms, while all those whose surfaces are sufficiently solid play host to sprawling hab complexes, manufactora and city-sized fortifications. An unending river of Humanity pours along the system's space lanes and fills its structures to capacity and beyond. It is amongst these masses that rebellion, sedition and heresy can and do foment.

It is, of course, the duty of the Inquisition to root out such threats, and indeed some of the Ordos' most zealous agents spend

their entire lives doing just that. However, even these pious Imperial servants are not immune to corruption, whether by nihilistic ideologues, Chaos taint or xenofanatical mesmerism.

Thus the Adeptus Custodes maintain their own presence, and perform their own patrols and monitoring sweeps throughout the Sol System. It is they who supervise the vetting of the countless Imperial citizens who pass through Terra's monolithic space ports every day. It is they who enact surprise sweeps and inspections of the Sol System's defences, following no set pattern or schedule beyond their own intuition to prevent any from predicting and avoiding their vigilance.

The Custodians seed listening devices, spy-servitors and dictalarcenous subroutines through the hives of the throneworld and beyond. They gather and analyse every scrap of information they can from even the darkest reaches of the Sol System, feeding ship names, population movements, labourers' shift schedules, demagogues' sermons, vox intercepts and more into macro-cogitators the size of battleships. The data prophecies that emerge from these vast engines aid the Captain-General in his command decisions on a daily basis, and help the Ten Thousand to be ever vigilant.

PHALANX

Ancient records suggest that, during the era of the Great Crusade, the Emperor travelled often aboard the immense, warp-capable battle station known as *Phalanx*. This was the flagship of the Imperial Fists, and remains their primary base of operations to this day. During the Horus Heresy that remarkable craft is believed to have hung above Terra, forming part of the world's defences. If this is so, then somehow it survived that cataclysmic conflict, and has endured the long millennia since.

Phalanx was almost destroyed during the fall of Cadia, first by a daemonic infestation that overran its decks during warp transit, and then by the prodigious firepower of traitor warships. The battle station persevered through all of these hazards, however, successfully bearing many faithful Imperial warriors back to the Sol System and resuming its time-honoured position in orbit above the throneworld.

Since then, repairs have been under way to restore *Phalanx* to its full functionality, and to purify those zones of the craft deemed tainted by the touch of Chaos. Amidst the endless bustle, the toing and froing of gene-bulked work gangs, and the interminable rites of the Ministorum, the Adeptus Custodes have had little difficulty seeding agents onto the craft.

Hidden in plain sight, these intruders keep careful watch over what they view as a dangerously potent Adeptus Astartes war engine, and stand ready to take whatever action they must. To the Custodians, even the most loyal Space Marine Chapters will always be potential traitors. It is their duty never to forgive, nor forget, what trust in the Primarchs led to. Thus, were *Phalanx* ever to direct its guns towards the Imperial Palace, the Custodians would enact veiled protocols that would see it scuttled before it could fire a shot.

TERRA & LUNA

PHALANX
[IMPERIAL FISTS
BATTLE FORTRESS]

HOLY TERRA
[THRONEWORLD]

Ω784Ẏ340
34ðX331
60211I90

LUNA
[CIVILISED/DEATH WORLD]

SEGMENTUM
OBSCURUS

ULTIMA
SEGMENTUM

SEGMENTUM
SOLAR

SOL SYSTEM &
HOLY TERRA

SEGMENTUM
TEMPESTUS

THE EASTERN FRINGE

SOL SYSTEM
+ CORE WORLDS SHOWN +

SATURN
[GAS GIANT]

MARS
[FORGE WORLD]

HOLY TERRA
[THRONEWORLD]

+ CLASSIFIED +
[ARTEFACT 9-KAPPA-MU]

VENUS
[INDUSTRIAL
WORLD]

MERCURY
[MINING WORLD]

JUPITER
[GAS MINING
WORLD]

Σ889T004
2DΔ1126
Ь55FX12

SEGMENTUM SOLAR

FENRIS

HYDRAPHUR

ELYSIA

PRESCIENCE
[ADEPTUS CUSTODES
STAR KEEP]

ARMAGEDDON

TALON AEGIS
[ADEPTUS CUSTODES
STAR KEEP]

Π57T68.Δ72.Π41MЬH112

ORACLE MAXIMUS
[ADEPTUS CUSTODES
STAR KEEP]

SOL

VORDRAST

EYRIE PRIME
[ADEPTUS CUSTODES
STAR KEEP]

GATHALAMOR

Ь752X119
5CÍ4582.
ẊX56NO88

NECROMUNDA

Δ04X27.Σ19Δ72.Π27MT04

DEIMOS
[FORGE WORLD]

TITAN
[GREY KNIGHTS
FORTRESS WORLD]

MIMAS
+ CLASSIFIED +

SATURN
[GAS GIANT]

IAPETUS
[NAVAL FORTRESS]

ENCELADUS
+ REDACTED +

TETHYS
[DEATH WORLD]

THE IRON RING

Δ068Ẏ963
Σ9HJ6349
Π85NQ49

PHOBOS
[ORBITAL FORTRESS]

MARS
[FORGE WORLD]

FERRUM RAPTORIS
[ADEPTUS CUSTODES
STAR KEEP]

SATURN & TITAN

MARS & PHOBOS

THE TALE OF THE TEN THOUSAND

From out of the mists of time stride the Adeptus Custodes. Their long path leads from the darkness of Old Night, through the fires of the Horus Heresy, and out of the shadows of ten thousand years of ignorant obfuscation into the cold light of the present. In all of those hundreds of centuries the Custodians have never faltered, and they never shall.

M30-M32 THE ERA OF GLORY AND SHAME

The Great Crusade

The Emperor unites all of Terra beneath his rule and strikes out into the galaxy at the head of his armies of unification. The Great Crusade sweeps through the void like a tidal wave, uniting the scattered worlds of Humanity and driving the xenos races into the shadows. The Emperor leads the greatest battles of this era in person, and always at his side stride the peerless warriors of the Legio Custodes. Clad in gleaming auramite, wielding blades that crackle with fell energies, the Ten Thousand cut down all that stand before them, and stamp Mankind's glorious authority upon the stars.

The Burning of Prospero

After the Triumph at Ullanor, the Emperor returns to Terra to apply himself to a task of utmost secrecy and importance. The Great Crusade continues under Warmaster Horus of the Luna Wolves, but dark powers are at work, attempting to pervert the favoured Primarch's rule and sow discord throughout the nascent Imperium. The first outward sign of the coming catastrophe is the Burning of Prospero. Magnus the Red, Primarch of the Thousand Sons, unleashes forbidden sorceries that wreak havoc upon Terra, though most will never know whether this act was one of aggression or an attempt to deliver a desperate warning of Horus' fall. In the end, the truth is immaterial; the Emperor unleashes a censure force under Constantin Valdor and Primarch Leman Russ of the Space Wolves, charged with apprehending Magnus on his home world of Prospero and returning him to Terra to answer for his acts. Matters escalate rapidly and the mission of capture becomes one of wholesale annihilation, Valdor and his Custodians fighting alongside the Space Wolves to overcome the sorcery of Magnus' sons.

The Horus Heresy

Warmaster Horus openly declares his allegiance to the Dark Gods of Chaos, leading fully half of his brother Primarchs and their Space Marine Legions in rebellion against the throne. War consumes the Imperium, a swift-spreading conflagration that threatens to turn to ash all the Emperor has built. Yet as his sons and their Legions battle across the stars, the Master of Mankind is nowhere to be seen. In truth, he and his Legio Custodes are engaged in their own desperate conflict, fighting upon a trans-dimensional battlefield the Emperor once sought to tame for Mankind's use. Tragically, this existential war keeps the Custodians from exacting the Emperor's vengeance upon his wayward sons – the Ten Thousand do not take a major role in the battle for the Imperium until the foe is beating at the very gates of the Emperor's palace.

An Unthinkable Cost

At the culmination of the Siege of Terra, the Emperor leads a last-ditch boarding action against Horus' battle barge, the *Vengeful Spirit*. He meets Horus in single combat and defeats him at last, but the cost is appalling. Though they cut down traitors and Daemons beyond count, the Legio Custodes are unable to prevent Horus from crippling the Emperor, and leaving his father's mind and soul trapped in a shattered husk of a body. Grief-stricken, the Custodians bear their master's body back to Terra, there to be interred forevermore within the machineries of the Golden Throne. They swear a penitent's oath and don the mourning black, consigning themselves to watching over their fallen lord for the rest of time.

A Legend's End

The Emperor's surviving loyal sons lead a furious war of vengeance, hounding the Traitor Legions across the galaxy. This period will come to be known as the Scouring, and it is a time of violent catharsis and retribution. Yet the newly reorganised Adeptus Custodes take no part in it, standing their sombre watch upon the throneworld and contemplating their ultimate failure. Though records conflict as to how and when, it is during this period that Captain-General Constantin Valdor disappears from Imperial histories, along with his weapons and armour, which never make their way to the Hall of Armaments. The Custodians elect Valdor's successor from amongst their ranks and continue their watch.

The War of the Beast

Still recovering from the events of the Horus Heresy, the Imperium is again beset. This time it is the Ork menace that almost overruns Mankind, bringing their war all the way to gates of Terra itself. Bound by oath and duty, the Custodians take little part in the sprawling conflict, save to strike down a force of Aeldari who attempt to cut a path to the Emperor's throne room during the chaos and confusion.

M33-M39 THE ERA OF VIGILANCE UNSTINTING

Siege of the Eternity Gate

Capitalising upon contacts within the Fartraders' Guild of the Yndonesic Hives, the Cult of the Hedonic Lord seize control of much of the Eternity Gate space port. Repeated attempts are made by the Adeptus Arbites to break the heretic barricades, but every attack is hurled back by tides of fanatics. Meanwhile, word escapes the space port that the cultists are repurposing hundreds of heavy landers and atmospheric barges for an all-out attack upon the Imperial Palace. Identifying the cult activity as now posing a direct threat to the Emperor's safety, a shield host of the Adeptus Custodes launches a blistering attack. Land Raiders and Venerable Contemptors smash through the cult's barricades, even as sleek squadrons of Vertus Praetors strike at the heretics from above. Bands of Custodians tear through the cultists with merciless efficiency, driving their victims before them and trapping them in macro-hangar level one-four-two. There the Cult of the Hedonic Lord are slaughtered to the last, and their deviant dreams of an attack upon the Golden Throne ground to dust.

Blood Will Tell

Leotydus Dat-Hastael runs a successful Blood Game, spending over a decade in hiding, evading every ward and sentry to finally reach the Sanctum Imperialis with blade in hand. Precautions are put in place to seal off his route of ingress, just in time to catch the elite Drukhari killer known as the Blade of Ptesh as he attempts the very same route as Dat-Hastael in his efforts to slay the Emperor on behalf of a mysterious and exceptionally persuasive patron. The Blade's ambitions, and indeed his life, meet a merciless end, though he refuses to the end to give up the identity of the one who sent him.

The Ominous Gift

Halo-belt augurs reveal the space hulk *Ominous Gift* advancing inexorably out of the dark void towards Terra. Using his status as a High Lord to overrule objections by the Imperial Navy, Captain-General Aesoth Koumadra orders a strike by several shield companies to gut the craft from the inside and ensure its corruption is wholly purged. Those outside the Adeptus Custodes do not understand the significance, but the attack is led by the Lockwarden of the Shadowkeepers and a band of his black-armoured comrades. The *Ominous Gift* is destroyed – the wider Imperium need never know any more than that.

Guardians of Greatness

A controversial act of insubordination sees Lieutenant Nathasian of the Cadian 86th slated for execution. Yet he is spared when a band of grim-faced Custodians from the Aquilan Shield appear at his side in a blaze of golden light, and wordlessly cut down his would-be commissariat executioners. With his remarkable bodyguards at his side, Nathasian is free to exercise his flair for unconventional tactics, which soon sees his promotion to Commander Army Group, then to Warmaster of an entire Imperial crusade. The Shuddering Stars are swept clear of Ork tribes, stopping Waaagh! Dakskrag in its tracks before it can descend

upon the Sol System. In the wake of Nathasian's triumph over the greenskins, his bodyguards depart as suddenly as they had arrived and – never ones to rescind a sentence – the commissariat see Warmaster Nathasian dead before the day is out.

M40-M41 THE ERA OF BALEFUL PREMONITIONS

Envoys to the Omnissiah

During Abaddon the Despoiler's eighth Black Crusade, a combined force of Night Lords and Iron Warriors captures the Andromax System and a direct threat to Terra is identified. Initially, the notoriously insular Fabricator-General Uixot of Mars refuses to pledge his aid in eliminating the Heretic Astartes. However, when a diplomatic mission from the Adeptus Custodes attends his forge-temple in person, the Fabricator-General's ego is stroked and his mind swayed. Mere months later, a combined force of Minotaurs Space Marines, Adeptus Mechanicus war maniples and Custodians from the Dread Host annihilates the traitors in their captured strongholds.

The Mind Thieves

For twenty years, Shield-Captain Tybanus Lencilius pieces together scattered clues until at last he unearths an insidious scheme by a conclave of radical Thorians to steal psykers destined for the Emperor's table and slowly starve the Master of Mankind. Sensing a deeper level still to this perfidy, Lencilius continues his investigations with cold, deliberate patience until at last he has concrete proof: the Inquisitors have struck a deal with High Lord Sennaca, who is contriving to hide their activities in exchange for being allowed to sell the stolen psykers on to wealthy nobles for exorbitant fees. At last the Shield-Captain is able to release his pent-up fury, assembling a combined force of Custodians, Sisters of Silence and Imperial assassins to pull the corrupt operation up by its roots. Neither the

Thorians nor Sennaca, nor any of his inner circle, survive the vengeful purge that follows.

The Years of Madness

A time of strange omens and ominous whispers engulfs Terra, beginning with the disappearance of the notoriously conservative Captain-General Galahoth. Battling the stagnation of Galahoth's rule, the Adeptus Custodes find themselves facing a shocking increase in cult activity – both heretical and xenophile – throughout the Sol System. Doomsday sects trigger queue-wars between the pilgrim tribes within the Emperor's palace itself, and the Custodians are forced to exercise their authority in the bloodiest fights they have seen in centuries. Reports from the Dark Cells cite a growing sense of agitation amongst the hidden inmates, and numerous support servitors have to be destroyed by the Shadowkeepers after they exhibit sudden, violent madness. Worse is to follow as possession is revealed amongst a sub-sect of the doomscryers themselves, though not until the false predictions of the fallen psykers send Captain-General Launceddre to his death at the Battle of the Gilded Pyre. It is amidst this climate of spiralling paranoia and danger that Captain-General Trajann Valoris is elevated to command the Ten Thousand, and he wastes no time in taking steps to regain ironclad control of Terra's defences.

To Stand Against the Storm

In the wake of Valoris' rise to power, the Adeptus Custodes enjoy their most proactive century of martial and covert action since the fall of Goge Vandire. They annihilate dozens of hidden cults, purge the polar underhives, eliminate a vermillion-classified xenos threat amidst the Plutonian void-fortresses, and launch thirty-two separate extrasolar interdiction strikes. Several, it is rumoured, even utilise shattered spars of the webway to reach their targets. As word reaches Terra of ever increasing warp storm activity, and cries for help sweep in from every corner of the galaxy, Valoris assembles the High Lords of Terra to discuss their response to this gathering storm. Yet it is at that moment that word reaches their closed session of an incredible disturbance on the surface of Luna, of demigods battling through the airless void at the head of great armies, and of a Primarch restored by the strangest of roads. Roboute Guilliman has returned, and Valoris knows that nothing will be the same ever again…

M41 THE ERA OF RELENTLESS AGGRESSION

The Battle of Lion's Gate

Barely has Roboute Guilliman returned to Terra when the empyric bow waves of the Great Rift sweep over the Sol System. Riding their boiling crests comes a horde of Khornate Daemons, who burst through the skin of reality to assail Terra itself. Though this is the Adeptus Custodes' nightmare scenario, they enact their Catastrophe Protocols with unshakeable calm and self-assurance. Storming out to meet the invaders alongside Guilliman's Ultramarines and a sizeable complement of Sisters of Silence, the Custodians successfully deflect the Blood God's attempt to behead the Imperium with a single strike. Victory is bought at a steep price in irreplaceable lives, but it is victory nonetheless.

In the battle's aftermath, Valoris and Guilliman quickly reach an agreement: the role of the Adeptus Custodes must change, for they can no longer effectively defend the Golden Throne from behind the palace ramparts alone.

Bringers of Greatness

Roboute Guilliman announces the Indomitus Crusade, a desperate and determined undertaking by a combined Imperial force to drive back the rampaging armies of Chaos. As part of this crusade, the Ultramarines Primarch intends to bear Primaris Space Marine reinforcements and the secrets behind their creation to the far-flung and hard-pressed Space Marine Chapters. On the eve of his decision, a large number of Emissaries Imperatus step forwards, compelled by the spirit of the Emperor to accompany the crusade. These will be the envoys who bring Guilliman's gift to the Adeptus Astartes; their presence will ensure that even those Chapters the Primarch does not visit in person understand the gravitas of what they are offered, and set aside whatever mistrust or conservatism they might have in order to embrace the Emperor's beneficence in their hour of need.

Carnage on Gathalamor Prime

The Gathalamor System comes under sustained attack from the Heretic Astartes of the Word Bearers Legion. As their Dark Apostles summon creatures from beyond the veil, the fight turns viciously against the Imperial defenders. The Mordian 84th and the Sisters of the Argent Shroud dig in to stage their last stand in the grim ruins of Gathalamor Prime's macro-cathedrum, their prayers for salvation ringing out to the screaming skies above. Sure enough, even as hordes of traitors and abominations mobilise to attack, the Emperor answers the cries of his followers. Teleport flares erupt through the heretic lines, gold and silver lightning leaping as a combined force of Custodians and Grey Knights storm into battle. Bolters roar and crackling blades tear through heretic flesh, Trajann Valoris and Grand Master Voldus leading an assault that sees the traitor army shattered into battling warbands.

Inspired by the sudden arrival of veritable demigods, the Mordians and Sisters of Battle advance, hymnals rising from their ranks over the roar of flamers and the scream of massed lasgun fire. Blood slicks the streets around the macro-cathedrum, corpses piling in gory heaps as the Word Bearers and their daemonic allies fight back furiously. Yet after three days and nights of unremitting savagery, the Chaos host is broken in the Battle for the Statue Steps. With fresh Imperial reinforcements flooding in to the wider Gathalamor war zone, the Custodians set course for Terra, leaving the Grey Knights to deal as they see fit with the unfortunates that they rescued from the macro-cathedrum.

Giants and Gods

Fighting alongside the Knights of House Krast, a shield company of the Adeptus Custodes storms the battle lines of the Necron tomb world of Trynnect. They smash through the android xenos and obliterate the cabal of Crypteks at its heart, thus preventing the awakening of the ancient star god Zul'channec within the northern bounds of the Segmentum Solar.

The Echovault

Led by the ambitious Chaos Lord Hadrexus, a sizeable contingent of Black Legionnaires fall upon the world of Dakhorth. They sweep aside the planet's defending regiments and advance to secure the ancient xenos ruin known as the Echovault. Before they can lay claim to this mysterious structure, two of the warships known as the *Moiraides* appear in orbit. The Custodians of the Dread Host deploy in force, securing the mountain pass that leads to the Echovault with squads of Wardens who hold firm against wave after wave of attacks. Meanwhile, multiple shield companies strike at the flanks of the traitor force, pulling their formation apart and dividing their strength. Finally, a decisive force of forty Allarus Terminators teleports into the very heart of the Black Legion lines, tearing their command structure apart and slaying Lord Hadrexus and his Chosen to the last. Though dozens of Custodians fall during the fighting, they smash the Black Legion invaders utterly and send their remnants fleeing back into the warp. As for the Echovault, it is left undisturbed, and a permanent garrison of Custodian Wardens left to watch over it.

The Dangers of Excellence

Amidst the horrors of the ongoing war against Chaos, it is deemed heresy for Administratum clerks to suggest the Adeptus Custodes could ever lose a battle, regardless of the odds. Fearing for their safety and their souls, many adepts record campaigns as Imperial victories even before the first shots are fired, should so much as a single Custodian be reported active in that war zone. Needless to say, more than one system is lost to subsequent disaster despite the Custodians' endeavours.

Vadrian's Quest

For millennia, the Adeptus Mechanicus has striven to maintain the esoteric technologies within the Golden Throne. Despite their best efforts, systems continue to fail, and no one still living knows how to repair them. Perceiving such dangerous ignorance as a manifest threat to the Emperor's safety – and thus falling beneath the purview of the Adeptus Custodes – Shield-Captain Heraclast Vadrian consults with Trajann Valoris and receives permission to seek a solution. He gathers a band of his finest warriors aboard the cruiser *Scion of Argo*, and sets off following a lead that points to the lost forge world of Morvane.

On the Plains of Pallus

Following the disastrous collapse of Lord Commander Ustrin's Victorium Crusade, heretic forces break through the Imperial lines on a system-wide scale. Their advance is spearheaded by the renegade armoured companies of the Vostokh 7th, led by the traitorous Marshal Griegor, whose battle tanks repel every Imperial force sent to stop them. At last, upon the rocky plains of Pallus, Griegor meets his match. Screaming into battle upon their ornate steeds come Shield-Captain Aadilus and his company of Vertus Praetors, melta missiles streaking from their salvo launchers to annihilate the lead vehicles of the Vostokh spearhead. The traitor tanks open fire with everything they have, seeking to swat the seemingly outmatched jetbikes from the air. Yet the Praetors weave effortlessly between the shots, weathering those blasts that do hit home and suffering only scant casualties before they split into hunting packs and begin criss-cross strafing runs over and between the enemy armour. More renegade vehicles explode by the moment, the Vostokh gunners panicking as they find themselves unable to track their hurtling tormentors. Like a shoal of razorfish, the Custodians pick apart their enemies, losing less than a third of their number as they annihilate the enemy's numerically superior army. Marshal Griegor's Shadowsword is the last vehicle slain, its immense main gun proving worse than useless against the agile and resilient Vertus Praetors who reduce it to molten wreckage in a matter of minutes.

Silent Crossing

Since the inexplicable escape of Cypher, the mysterious Fallen Angel, from a high-security cell in the Imperial Palace, the Custodians charged with apprehending him have tirelessly attempted to reacquire their captive. Unable to find him on Terra, and following a trail of fading clues, Shield-Captain Daryth and his men have pressed out into the stars to continue their mission. Now they enlist the aid of the Sisters of Silence, bringing a band of the elite witch hunters aboard their frigate, *Sol's Arrow*, before making the perilous crossing of the Great Rift. The presence of the Silent Sisters seems to calm the madness of the empyrean, at least enough to aid the Custodians in making their dangerous journey into the Imperium Nihilus. Amidst the madness, their augurs do not detect the heavily shielded Space Marine cruiser that follows in their wake, its hull night-black and its insignia veiled.

The Osseous Tower Falls

The Haemonculi of the Twisted Spiral raise a vast bone fortress to float amidst the gaseous atmosphere of Othana V in the Vordrast System. As their raiding skiffs strike at the planet's gas-mining platforms – which directly serve Adeptus Custodes star keep Prescience – it is clear the threat cannot be ignored. Several shield companies launch strikes against the xenos, with the Allarus Custodians of the Gilded Fist leading the attack. Teleporting into the nightmarish Osseous Tower, they overcome every fiend and abomination that assails them, before destroying the tower's gravitic membranes and sending it tumbling down to be crushed in Neptune's high-pressure depths. The surviving Drukhari flee aboard sleek warships that swiftly vanish, while the Custodians evacuate in good order. Disquiet spreads, however, when several Custodians are found to be missing without trace at battle's end.

The Wyrmslayers

A Genestealer Cult calling themselves the Wyrms of the Ur-tendril are discovered by Ordo Xenos agents, entrenched amongst the Nordafrik under-archives on Terra. Captain-General Valoris refuses a request by the Deathwatch to send Kill Teams against this threat, instead leading the purge in person at the head of a huge Adeptus Custodes shield host. The Cult put up a brutal fight, their sheer numbers and fanaticism allowing them to drag down one Custodian after another and tear them limb from limb. Yet for every one of the Custodians that falls, hundreds upon hundreds of malformed cultists and Aberrants are slaughtered. At last, Valoris himself beheads the monstrous Broodlord that ruled over the cult. He orders the creature's disturbing inner sanctum burned despite the protests from the Ordo Xenos investigators – Valoris refuses to let anyone other than his comrades witness the foul mural that decorates the sanctum's back wall, of a nest of fanged tendrils emerging from the heart of Sol itself to devour Terra whole…

Zagstomp's Doom

The Orks of Waaagh! Zagstomp overrun the Iron Warriors Citadel of Miseries after a gruelling three-year siege. Grown massive and powerful on a diet of constant warfare, and equipped with the looted tanks and war engines of the butchered Iron Warriors, Zagstomp's hordes board their ramshackle ships. Before they can attempt to punch their way into the warp, Custodians of the Solar Watch materialise within the engine decks and mek bays of the greenskins' capital ships. Guns blazing, the Custodians hold off the Orks long enough to plant vortex implosion detonators on every ship. The survivors then teleport back to their own ships and jump away into the warp. In attempting to give chase, the Orks trigger the vortex bombs, and their vast fleet – which Imperial doomscryers warned would appear on the fringes of the Sol System if left unchecked – is consumed by the ferocious energy storm that follows.

Duty unto Death

Amidst the shadows of the Imperium Nihilus, a small Imperial fleet finds itself beset by a pair of wayward Tyranid hive ships. The Imperial flagship, the *Terra Nostra*, is transporting Primaris gene-tech under the protection of Custodian Wardens. Seeing that the fleet will soon be overrun, the guardians' Shield-Captain orders an emergency teleport to the nearby death world of Loqe II. Pursued by Tyranid swarms, the Wardens retreat into the fume-choked volcanic highlands and prepare to defend their precious cargo to the last. Wave after wave of Tyranids surge up the perilous lava-channels, but the Custodians – cleaving to their oaths of indomitable defence – repulse every attack.

A month later, a relief force of Marines Malevolent arrives in orbit and drives the hive ships away with thunderous firepower. On the planet below they find a single living Warden, grievously wounded yet still standing guard over the untouched boon of technology amidst a fortress of heaped Tyranid corpses.

Into Shadow

Upon the direct orders of Trajann Valoris, a small, fast-moving force of Custodians makes haste for the ruined remains of Cadia. Details of their mission are suppressed, even amongst their comrades, but they are accompanied by a number of warriors drawn from the ranks of the Shadowkeepers.

With gilded blade and thundering bolter did the Ten Thousand march out to meet Waaagh! Deffbringa. Before the gates of the Petitioner's Fortress upon sainted Argentum, no less than eight shield hosts marched as one. Like the Emperor's own blade they thrust deep into the Ork horde, and with a single unstoppable blow they pierced its heart.

CAPTAIN-GENERAL TRAJANN VALORIS

CHIEF CUSTODIAN, FIRST OF THE TEN THOUSAND

The office of Captain-General is one of the most powerful military appointments in the Imperium. It confers full responsibility for the overall defence of the Sol System, Terra, the Imperial Palace and – ultimately – the Golden Throne and the Emperor himself. The Captain-General is the master of the Adeptus Custodes, and, on many occasions during Imperial history, has stood amongst the ranks of the High Lords of Terra. He is further charged with leading the greatest military campaigns fought by the Ten Thousand, and must display a degree of warrior prowess that approaches that of the Primarchs of old.

In the millennia since the Great Crusade, there have been just seventeen incumbents of this weighty mantle. Most have died in battle, either on the holy soil of Terra or whilst leading crucial campaigns amidst the stars. Several have become Eyes of the Emperor, while three – including Constantin Valdor himself – simply vanished, their disappearances wreathed in mystery even amongst their own comrades.

The current Captain-General is Trajann Valoris. Many claim that he is the greatest warrior to hold the title since the Emperor bestrode the stars. Within his first decade of service, Valoris ran not just one, but two successful Blood Games, a record that remains unbroken. With his remarkable grasp of battlefield strategy and his naturally aggressive streak he earned a place for himself amongst the

Allarus Custodians. There, Valoris won many names from deeds such as the destruction of the space hulk *Mournful Siren*, the defeat of the Genestealer Cult of the Emperor's Writhing Shadow, and his spearheading of the preemptive strike against Waaagh! Krushfist.

If Valoris showed a weakness, it was his reluctance to stand back and wait for his enemies to come to him. He lasted only twenty-two years amongst the Companions before his desire to participate in a more proactive strategy of defence saw him reassigned. He gained the rank of Shield-Captain soon afterwards, and spent several centuries leading sorties against emergent threats throughout the Sol System and beyond. Valoris became well known for his tendency to observe his enemies carefully, predict their movements, then deliver a sudden and decisive blow. He cultivated networks of agents and informers across the Segmentum Solar, and even further out into the wider Imperium. Valoris recognised his own proclivity for aggressive action, and took constant steps to temper it with comprehensive foreknowledge. Thus his strikes always fell where they should, and no comrade was ever lost to reckless commands.

When Captain-General Andros Launceddre fell at the Battle of the Black Pyre, Valoris was named his successor. As tradition dictated, he took up the armour and weapons of his former lord. These masterfully crafted artefacts were fashioned in the wake of Constantin Valdor's disappearance and passed on to each new Captain-General ever since. The first is the Watcher's Axe, a huge polearm blade that crackles with golden lightning and can bisect the sarcophagus of a Chaos Helbrute with a single swing. The axe's haft incorporates a master-crafted bolt weapon known as the Eagle's Scream, which fires adamantium-tipped penetrator bolts at a ferocious rate.

The second of these great relics is an elaborate suit of powered armour known as the Castellan Plate, which incorporates a heraldic tilting shield, an auramite halo, and a magnificent cloak woven with adamantine thread so that it flows like cloth but yields to neither blade nor blast. At his belt the Captain-General also carries a strange device known as the Moment Shackle. A relic of Dark Age technology released from the vaults beneath the Imperial Palace, this artefact allows Valoris to trap fragments of temporal energy and turn them to his use, excising split-second events from history or slowing the localised temporal flow enough to tip a desperate fight in his favour.

Trajann Valoris has proven a dynamic and effective Captain-General. Under his rule the number of Blood Games have increased tenfold, the defences of the stable warp routes into the Sol System have been strengthened, and long-hidden cults have been purged from the Terran underhives. Little escapes the eyes of his ever expanding spy network and, armed with the certainty of the truly righteous, his covert strikes have annihilated dozens of threats to the Golden Throne. It was as if Valoris had foreseen Guilliman's return and the Great Rift long before they came, and laid all the groundwork required for the Adeptus Custodes to adapt to the new Imperium. Perhaps, some whispered, the half-understood power of the Moment Shackle allowed him to do just that. Whatever the case, the Captain-General's many qualities make him ideally suited to lead in this age of unprecedented aggression.

SHIELD-CAPTAINS

The warriors of the Adeptus Custodes disregard the idea of blind obedience, and look with disdain upon those who follow the orders of their superiors without question. After all, it was this very practice within the Legiones Astartes that allowed the Horus Heresy to occur. Every Custodian has a voice, and is expected to use it. As such, the Ten Thousand respect only those leaders who have proved themselves worthy, whose judgement, strategic skill and strength of mind and character have been shown time and again. Such Custodians are called Shield-Captains, and their fellows follow them with loyalty and dedication.

Shield-Captains are amongst the greatest assets of the Imperium. They are superlative warriors who are able to take on an entire squad of Heretic Astartes in close combat, strike the heads from xenos beasts the size of tanks, and fell rank after rank of lesser enemies with pinpoint fire. Whether they hack their enemies apart with powerful swings of a castellan axe, slice and stab with a sentinel blade, or impale their victims upon a crackling guardian spear, Shield-Captains display absolute mastery of their chosen weapons. Some – the swiftest in thought and action – soar into battle in the saddle of a Dawneagle jetbike. Others – those of an especially bellicose and aggressive temperament – favour teleporting to war clad in Allarus Terminator armour, there to cut down the enemy's leaders and send their underlings fleeing in terror. Whatever their preference, Shield-Captains are the masters of those disciplines required to become heroes of legend.

More than just exceptional fighters, Shield-Captains are highly intelligent and tactically gifted battlefield commanders, able to read the ebb and flow of the wider war at a glance and direct their forces accordingly. A great weight of responsibility is placed upon the shoulders of these warrior lords, for to squander the Emperor's personal guards is an unforgivable sin. They know neither fear nor self-doubt, and can appear arrogant and aloof to other warriors of the Imperium. This is a misconception, however, for Shield-Captains are untroubled by such self-serving notions as egotism. They are absolute realists, fully aware of the stakes involved in the wars they wage. They act accordingly, every statement declarative, every action decisive, suffering no impediment to their mission – be it the machinations of the foe or the pomposity, ignorance or superstition of their allies.

This is not to say that Shield-Captains lack for charisma. Rather, they exude it. To the common soldiery of the Imperium these gilded figures seem to have stepped from the pages of religious scripture. Their presence fills faithful men and women with rapturous euphoria, banishing fears and doubts, replacing them with the absolute certainty that the Emperor watches over his servants and will preserve their souls should they fall in battle that day. Shield-Captains are also master diplomats, well versed in the intricacies of Imperial high society, privy to secrets and traditions that allow them to charm, inspire, threaten and manipulate as required to see their will done.

The rank of Shield-Captain is a purely martial one. It signifies that the Custodian in question has the responsibility of leading a force of his comrades into battle. Beneath that umbrella honorific are hundreds of more symbolic or traditional titles. Some are retained only as long as a duty or position is fulfilled, while others are kept in perpetuity. Titles such as Aquila Commander, Justus Supreme or Emperor's Headsman are amongst the former, and correspond to guardianship of sections of the Imperial Palace or duties upon the field of battle. Conversely, a Custodian who has stood amongst the Companions will forever be known as Honoured Watchman, while one who has triumphed in a Blood Game will forever after bear the title of Shieldsmith.

When the Custodians march to war, it is not unusual to see multiple Shield-Captains leading them in battle. Sometimes these warriors fight alongside each other – groupings such as the Golden Brothers or the Heralds Three have won remarkable renown through their impressive accomplishments. At other times, one amongst the Shield-Captains' number will assume overall command of an especially important mission, his peers lending him their martial prowess and strategic counsel. The decision of who leads at such times is rarely difficult, for the Shield-Captains are frank in discussing their respective merits and quick to recognise whether they, or one of their fellows, is the appropriate choice. So do Shield-Captains epitomise their organisation's pragmatic approach to achieving victory in the Emperor's name.

CUSTODIANS

The Adeptus Custodes are the Emperor's vengeance made manifest. They defend the Master of Mankind with singular determination and breathtaking skill, and whether their vigil requires them to stand immovable before the gates of the Imperial Palace or storm into battle on a distant alien world, they do their duty without a moment's hesitation.

CUSTODIAN GUARD

When shield companies of the Adeptus Custodes strike out to do battle with the enemies of Mankind, it is the Custodian Guard that form their backbone. These warriors are rank-and-file infantry only insomuch as their numbers are greater than those of the other, more specialised Adeptus Custodes warriors. Even a single one of their number is a terrifying force of destruction, his every shot perfectly placed, his every cut, thrust and stab a masterclass in bladesmanship, footwork and combat awareness that sees enemy corpses fall like dead leaves at his feet. Ferociously strong, phenomenally resilient, utterly without fear or doubt, the Custodian Guard are the equal of many foes' most elite warriors.

Custodian Guard are steadfast in defence and unstoppable on the attack. Such squads do not have formal memberships, and Custodians may swap from one squad to another before each new campaign, or even each new battle. With their individualistic fighting styles, the Custodian Guard do not fight as one in the way that a conventional squad of soldiers would – it is enough for them to know that they fight shoulder to shoulder with respected comrades, and that their fellows will watch their backs when the enemy press close.

As with all of the Adeptus Custodes, Custodian Guard have the might of the Emperor flowing through their veins, and his aegis of protection hanging around them like a shield. Their traditional armament is the guardian spear, a golden halberd so heavy it would take several men to lift it. This composite weapon is both a powered blade capable of hewing a Chaos Space Marine in two, and a boltgun to engage threats from afar. Conversely, some Custodian Guard prefer to enter battle armed with a sentinel blade and storm shield. The sentinel blade is a broadsword of daunting size, so large its hilt is flanked with the double barrels of a bolt caster that can lay down a hail of short-range fire. It is a testament to the strength of the Custodians that they can wield these powered blades one-handed. When coupled with the armoured bulwark of the storm shield – whose protective powers are augmented with an inbuilt energy-shield generator – this potent combination allows the Custodian Guard to cut their foes apart while weathering even the most devastating of attacks.

As befits their elevated status, Custodian Guard squads can call upon ancient Land Raider battle tanks to carry them to war. The combination of demigod-like warriors and enormous war engine is a terrifyingly potent one, and when several such squads advance at once, even super-heavy armour and towering daemonic abominations cannot endure their wrath.

CUSTODIAN WARDENS

Custodian Wardens can be recognised by the ceremonial robes that they wear over their armour. These are a mark of their veteran status, for every Custodian Warden has seen at least five centuries in the Emperor's service.

Those Wardens that do not carry the iconic guardian spears of their order wield heavy-bladed castellan axes. These weapons lend themselves to an elegant and brutal combat style that sees the wielder use their exceptional strength in conjunction with their axe's momentum, launching thunderous sweeps that switch direction with breathtaking suddenness to cleave through their victims' guard and hack off heads and limbs. The Wardens can also fire concentrated volleys of bolt fire from the hafts of their weapons, scything down those who attempt to stay out of their blades' devastating reach.

The Wardens are known amongst their comrades as level-headed and endlessly patient watchmen. Upon accepting the robes that mark their station they swear binding oaths to fight as immovable sentinels, a living fortress of auramite and sinew that no foe will ever breach. Each Warden's oaths are personal, written by the Custodian himself after a full year's contemplation sat in meditation upon the precipitous ledges of the Gallowtower. To break their vows would be worse than death to these warriors, and their determination to uphold them bolsters their already formidable wills to something of truly frightening intensity.

ALLARUS CUSTODIANS

The Allarus Custodians deploy with sudden fury to tear the throat from the enemy army. Where a strongpoint must be cracked wide open, a traitor warship boarded or a foul demagogue slain even as he stands amidst his dedicated bodyguards, there are the Allarus Custodians deployed.

These warriors wear suits of Allarus Terminator plate, expertly crafted armour whose worth can be measured in worlds. Driven by magnatomic generator-shrines, articulated with leonus-class actuators, and fashioned from layered auramite and adamantium, Allarus armour is a marvel of craftsmanship. It provides its wearer with an exceptional range of movement and near-unencumbered speed, augmented strength and resilience, and the survivability to stride unharmed from the blast of a macro-cannon shell. Coupled with the protective blessings of the Emperor, Allarus Terminator plate is arguably the most effective man-portable combat armour in the entire Imperium. Just as well, for the battles fought by Allarus Custodians demand nothing less.

Their weapons, too, are formidable. They heft guardian spears twice the height of a man, or swing massive castellan axes that can bisect a Chaos Lord or lop the head from an Ork psyker with a single blow. To supplement these weapons, Allarus Custodians also wield balistus grenade launchers upon their left forearms. These drum-fed weapons can be triggered with a thought, spitting salvoes of sanctified projectiles in saturation patterns through the enemy ranks. They are also capable of launching concussion grenades that explode amidst bursts of electroexorcist chaff and overwhelming light and sound. Enemies subjected to these barrages are sent reeling, their senses rebelling against the onslaught even as their weapons and equipment falter and they spasm in pain. Such armaments allow Allarus Custodians to suppress and then swiftly slaughter their target's bodyguards, leaving their true quarry exposed in the face of their wrath.

Hand-picked by the Captain-General from amongst the most bellicose of the Ten Thousand, Allarus Custodians relish the chance to plunge into the most lethal battles. Their killer instincts are razor-sharp, their wrath honed to a fine point. Yet these are no maniacal berserkers. Where many of the galaxy's most dangerous close-combat specialists allow their rage to drive them, Allarus Custodians leash their aggression wholly to their will. They land every blow with murderous strength, but also with surgical precision.

So aggressive and heroic are these warriors that, when the situation demands, they have been known to splinter their units entirely after the initial strike and scatter through the enemy's rear lines. Fighting as lone figures, the Allarus Custodians eliminate key targets, sow anarchy and confusion through unsuspecting forces, and completely destabilise the foe's formation before fresh Adeptus Custodes forces arrive to end the conflict. It is an effective tactic that has seen more than one heretic fortress fall from within.

THE GILDED FIST

In recent years, one band of Allarus Custodians has become renowned for their skill as terror troops and executioners. Known as the Gilded Fist, led by the indomitable Custodian Vanius Arcturon-Tybus, this squad has achieved remarkable feats of violence in the Emperor's name. It was the Gilded Fist who struck the head from the Ulgwyrm Cult of the Pan-Siberic Cluster, ended the insane machinations of Inquisitor D'anloxtos and led the purge of the traitor-held space hulk *Leviathan of Agonies* before it could reach the edge of the Sol System. Unusually for Custodians, these warriors have fought side by side for decades now, asserting that they can best serve the Emperor operating as a single, tightly fraternal force. With such renowned members as Manastus Chaem, Parradon Helastes and Dalat Hap-Uramedes fighting shoulder to shoulder to bring low the Emperor's foes, few can doubt the veracity of this claim.

VEXILUS PRAETORS

The Adeptus Custodes are a glorious and much celebrated force. In the earliest days of the Imperium they marched to war alongside the Emperor himself, presenting a magnificent spectacle which echoed the majesty of the Master of Mankind. Just as their weapons and armour have always been fashioned to reflect his martial glory, so too are the proud standards known as vexillas, which are borne to war by some of the most veteran Custodians.

Each vexilla is a towering banner topped with the Imperial Aquila, the ultimate symbol of the Emperor's authority. The Custodes alone are permitted to display it as their foremost heraldic icon, and its inspirational effect upon those around them is nothing short of electric. Hefted high above the anarchy of the battlefield, the vexilla forms a golden beacon of truth and light that fills true servants of the Emperor with awe. Beneath the winged shadow of the Aquila, even the humblest defender of Humanity feels the touch of the Emperor upon their soul. Meanwhile, the enemies of the Imperium cower in dismay; dread clouds their minds and saps their strength at the thought that the Emperor's greatest warriors are poised to tear them apart.

Each vexilla is created on Terra, painstakingly fashioned over a period of one hundred years by the oath-sworn artisans of the Tower Aquilane. Upon their completion, these beautiful standards are borne amidst processions of craft-thralls, Ministorum Priests and heraldic servitors to the Auric Eyrie, where they are held upon stasis-podia until required. Some vexillas are purely ritual in purpose, and are carried in procession and parade through the endless leagues of the Emperor's palace. Most, however, incorporate potent technologies suited specifically for deployment upon the field of battle.

Those vexillas carried by the veterans of the shield companies typically belong to one of several patterns. More than just standards to inspire adulation or terror, their inbuilt technologies provide invaluable battlefield support to the Custodians fighting in their shadow. Most common is the Vexilla Imperius, the mere presence of which

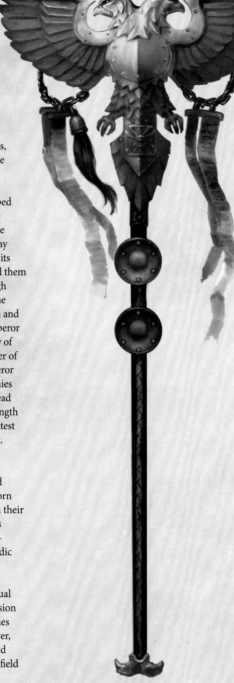

fills nearby Custodians with inviolable determination and lends fresh strength to their limbs. Whether this effect is purely psychological, or if there is some crypto-technological aspect to the phenomenon, is unknown beyond the Tower Aquilane. It is enough that it works, and works well.

The Vexilla Defensor is borne into battle where the foe brings overwhelming firepower to bear. Built into this proud standard is a refractor-field generator of prodigious power, whose protective umbrella crackles out to ward all nearby allied forces from harm. The deployment of these vexillas has spawned more than one legend and parable; to the unenlightened, the effects of the Vexilla Defensor look as though the Emperor is extending direct protection to those who fight at the side of his favoured warriors.

The Vexilla Magnifica incorporates photophantasmic fluctuators and psycho-amplifactor clarions. Those who dare to assail its bearer or his comrades find themselves blinded by the searing radiance of the Emperor's glory, their gunsights rebelling and their optic nerves burned out even as their thought patterns are smashed to fractal shards. Such standards are borne at the forefront of an attack, placed where they can best blunt any attempt by the foe to launch a counter-offensive of their own.

In addition to these technological marvels, all vexillas incorporate empyrically hardened teleport homers. These are most commonly used by the Adeptus Custodes to call in sudden strikes by fresh waves of Custodians, or, on rare occasions, even summon a Contemptor Dreadnought or Land Raider from the especially large, ancient and powerful Godstrike-pattern teleportariums aboard their warships. Whether blunting the enemy's sudden assault, exploiting a breakthrough in the foe's lines, or wrong-footing their victims with a sudden shift in the flow of the battle, such technology has many uses for the Ten Thousand, and fits perfectly with their style of warfare. Combined with the inspirational effect they have upon allied Imperial forces, and the Vexilus Praetor's own veteran combat skill, it is easy to see why few shield companies march to war without vexillas rising proud above them.

Not only do vexillas appear physically distinct, they also beam a constantly cycling set of data-ident codes that convey strategic information with friendly Imperial forces, and aid in tactical coordination.

VERTUS PRAETORS

Squads of Vertus Praetors swoop into battle astride powerful Dawneagle jetbikes. Veteran warriors who have seen battle on a hundred worlds, these Custodians know the true value of speed: not simply to bring the enemy to battle, but to direct their might precisely where and when it is needed most. Wherever they see their comrades hardest pressed, there the Vertus Praetors strike like golden lightning to bolster them.

These airborne warriors act as the eyes and ears of their shield companies, soaring over the battlefield and voxing word of the enemy's movements. Their auto-senses are optimised for this task, boasting suites of data-augurs, optical auspicators and multi-spectral motion-oracles that allow them to detect and track even hidden foes. With a squadron of sharp-eyed Vertus Praetors circling overhead, a Shield-Captain can rest assured the enemy stands little chance of catching him unawares.

Each Vertus Praetor is a master combatant who has already honed his superhuman skills amongst the ranks of the Custodian Guard. They are expert marksmen, able to place perfect kill shots even while screaming at breakneck pace through tangled ruins or dense forests. Their close-quarters prowess is no less exceptional; a Vertus Praetor can open the throat of a heavily armoured foe in a single pass. They can analyse even the most chaotic conflict in a heartbeat, reacting with incredible speed to evade obstacles and run down their foes, processing battlefield developments with breathtaking rapidity.

The exceptional skill of the Vertus Praetors is augmented by their superlative wargear. As well as being protected by auramite armour, these warriors wield enormous interceptor lances. Taller end-to-end than an Ogryn, and perfectly weighted, these fearsome weapons boast adamantium blades wreathed in disruptor fields. Vertus Praetors are masters of hit-and-run strikes, driving their lances clean through their precisely chosen targets before ripping them clear again as they speed past. The result is as devastatingly effective as it is explosively gory.

The greatest assets at the Vertus Praetors' disposal, however, are their mounts. The Dawneagle jetbike is an incredible vehicle, a crusade-era relic wrought in auramite and adamantium. These bikes are almost as large as light fighter craft and – while they are still grav-skimmers – can deliver a near supersonic turn of speed. Their hulls are phenomenally durable, allowing their riders to slam through walls and enemy warriors without being unseated, and they react pugnaciously to the slightest touch of the controls, able to jink effortlessly through incoming fire. When armed with hurricane bolters, the Dawneagle can plough bloody furrows through enemy hordes. However, it is when equipped with salvo launchers that Vertus Praetors truly come into their own as lightning-fast tank hunters. They scream across the battlefield, rapidly outflanking and encircling the heaviest enemy vehicles before annihilating them with strafing runs of melta missiles. Even enemy aircraft are not safe, for by combining their fire the Vertus Praetors are able to weave airborne webs of flakk blasts into which hurtling enemy aircraft slam with terminal results.

VENERABLE CONTEMPTOR DREADNOUGHTS

Bellowing a vox-amplified war cry, the Venerable Contemptor Dreadnought storms into the enemy with merciless fury. Heavy fire spits from its gun arm – either blasts of melta energy that reduce tanks to molten ruin or screaming hails of shells from the spinning barrels of the Kheres-pattern assault cannon. The Dreadnought's other arm ends in a fist like a wrecking ball, a gilded gauntlet that can tear the turret from a battle tank or splinter every bone in a body with a single punch. Wielding these weapons with a matchless skill characteristic of the Adeptus Custodes, the Contemptor blazes a trail of death and destruction through its enemies, tearing the heart from those who would stand against the Emperor and sending the terrified survivors fleeing in terror.

Each Venerable Contemptor Dreadnought is an ancient war engine, a relic that incorporates wonders of technology that the Imperium can no longer replicate. Its auramite armour plates are expertly crafted and maintained. Its limbs are articulated by fibre-bundles and servo-motors that afford it immense strength. Its weapons are perfectly calibrated, while its hull is sheathed in the crackling energies of an atomantic shield that can dispel laser blasts and artillery shells amidst bright flares of energy. Auto-repair protocols allow the Dreadnought to shrug off crippling battle damage, while motive shrines and auto-sanctified backup systems stand ready to take the strain should the Contemptor undergo serious combat trauma. Yet for all this arcane technology, the most important component of the Venerable Contemptor Dreadnought is the living warrior interred in the sarcophagus at its heart.

Though the physiology of the Custodians is remarkably durable, still there are wounds so severe that even they cannot survive them. When faced with certain death, a Custodian may choose to be preserved within a Venerable Contemptor Dreadnought so that he can continue to fight for the Emperor. There should be no mistaking that this is the act of a martyr, for life within a Dreadnought sarcophagus – even one as advanced as the Venerable Contemptor – is a twilight existence at best. The pilot is shorn of all unnecessary flesh, rendered down to little more than a sack of organs and brain matter sustained within an armaglass amniotic tank. They are then permanently fused with the life-support systems of the Dreadnought. Its powerful limbs become theirs to operate. Its complex sensoria become their eyes and ears, its vox emitter their mouth. The Custodian becomes a god of war, able to stride unharmed through hails of fire and crush the Master of Mankind's foes with their hydraulic might. In return, they face an eternity cut off from the outside world, bound to mechanical systems that can never truly replicate the feel of sunlight upon their skin, or the satisfying crunch of their blade through an enemy's flesh.

Despite this, there are tales of unharmed Custodians volunteering to pilot Contemptors whose previous occupants were slain in battle. Those soon to depart as Eyes of the Emperor, those who feel they have dishonoured themselves, even warriors who simply will not turn aside from what they perceive as their duty; all, it is said, have given their flesh willingly so that the Contemptor Dreadnoughts of the Custodes continue to stride to war.

Shield-Captain Hasturias Calaxor first took up the mantle of command during the Siege of Terra, the last, great battle of the Horus Heresy. It was Calaxor who held the Enlightener's Stair single-handedly against the turncoat soldiers of the 9th Terran Wardens. It was he that rallied the Gospodor Heavy Infantry with his inspiring example of bravery, and led them to retake the Dome of the Architects from Dortha Kol's Sons of Horus Legionaries. Joining forces with a sodality of his fellow Custodian Guard, it was Calaxor who finally drove Kol's warriors to destruction and felled the traitor Warhound Titan *Warp Jackal* into the bargain.

These heroics were enough to see Calaxor promoted amidst the fires of battle to the rank of Shield-Captain, after which he led three further highly successful counter-offensives before the siege's end. Renowned for the controlled aggression of his tactics, Calaxor earned himself many more names in the centuries that followed. On Thade,

he felled the Daemon Thogralathrax and prevented the Suppurant Scourge from being loosed on Terra. During the battle for the star keep Magnificence, Shield-Captain Calaxor went blade-to-blade with the heretical Singer of Miseries, before mounting his jetbike and leading a band of Vertus Praetors to end the traitor threat. It was Calaxor, also, whose blade ended the threat of the rogue assassin Shae before she could come within a hundred miles of the Golden Throne.

When the Shield-Captain finally fell in battle on the dead world of Palathrix, his sheer force of will kept him alive long enough to be interred within a Dreadnought sarcophagus. Becoming Venerable Ancient Calaxor, he assumed a new role within the Ten Thousand. Now Calaxor is a living war engine and strategic advisor both amidst the ranks of the Adeptus Custodes.

VENERABLE LAND RAIDERS

The Land Raider is arguably the most powerful and versatile battle tank available to Imperial forces in the 41st Millennium. Possessed of a fearsome array of weapons, hyper-durable adamantium armour, and the transport capacity to bear a full squad of heavily equipped warriors into battle, the Land Raider can function as both war engine and assault transport with equal ease. A single Land Raider can turn a desperate battle in the Imperium's favour – a massed spearhead of them can win a war.

For all this, Land Raiders are in comparatively short supply. Few forge worlds still possess the secrets of their creation, and even those that do must sink enormous resource and time into the making of each one. Land Raiders have bellicose and complex machine spirits that take time to tame, and for the material cost of but one of these tanks it is possible to churn out a hundred lesser vehicles. Every Land Raider is thus venerated as a priceless relic, entrusted only to the most elite forces of the Imperium and deployed when victory is absolutely vital. It is considered a near-irredeemable sin to allow such a vehicle to be destroyed, and entire campaigns have been fought to recover Land Raiders lost upon the field of battle.

The most ancient and honoured of these tanks are the Venerable Land Raiders used by the Adeptus Custodes. Many can trace their history all the way back to the earliest days of the Imperium. These tanks rolled forwards amidst the earth-shaking armoured spearheads deployed during the Great Crusade. They ground alien oppressors beneath their treads as they fought to liberate Humanity from the horrors of Old Night, and turned their guns mercilessly upon the Traitor Legions once their betrayal was revealed. For ten thousand years these noble war engines have fought for the Imperium, and each has built a legend every bit as magnificent as those possessed by the greatest Imperial champions.

Venerable Land Raiders possess Magos-class machine spirits, noble and aggressive entities that can independently aim and fire the tank's guns and coordinate its auto-repair rituals when circumstances require it. Stories exist of these dauntless war engines fighting on even after their Custodian crews were slain, wreaking bloody revenge for their deaths.

These vehicles are the primary ground transport of the Adeptus Custodes, a statement of how unstoppable and elite the Ten Thousand truly are. Tracks churning, guns thundering, Venerable Land Raiders ferry their passengers into the heart of battle, then support them with unparalleled armoured might once they disembark. In extreme circumstances these amazing war engines have even been teleported directly onto the battlefield, their hulls warded against the empyric corruption that is a common side effect of travelling through the warp, their passage assured through use of an ancient Godstrike-pattern teleportarium. This tactic has won many victories for the Adeptus Custodes; it is a rare enemy indeed that can survive the sudden appearance of a Land Raider full of demigods in the middle of their battle lines.

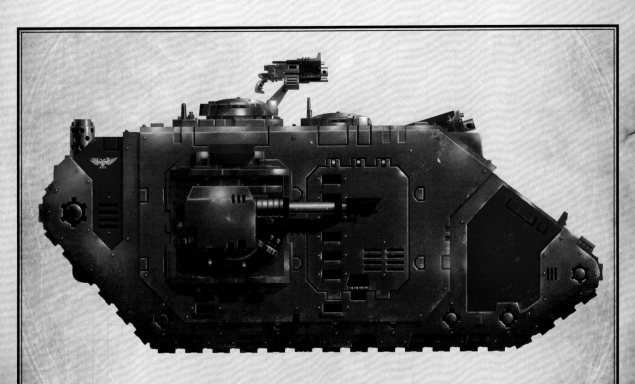

Pictured above is the Venerable Land Raider *Glory to the Throne*. This potent war engine saw its very first battle in the defence of the Emperor's palace at the culmination of the Horus Heresy. Though severely damaged during that apocalyptic conflict, *Glory to the Throne* has remained with the Adeptus Custodes ever since, repaired time and again, and blooded on battlefields beyond count.

THE SPLENDOUR OF HOLY TERRA

The Custodians take to the battlefield in compact, elite forces of highly trained warriors. They make for a spectacular sight with their gilded armour and gloriously worked wargear, proud vexillas rising over their lines. Yet to the Emperor's enemies, they are the terror of death incarnate.

Captain-General Trajann Valoris

The assembled might of the Adeptus Custodes surges into battle. Led by their heroic Captain-General and a band of redoubtable Allarus Custodians, they crash into the Death Guard lines like the Emperor's vengeance made manifest.

Led by formidable Allarus Custodians, a glorious host of the Adeptus Custodes surge into battle against the heretical warrior golems of the Thousand Sons Traitor Legion.

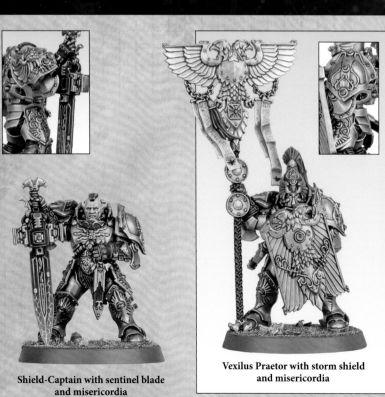

Shield-Captain with sentinel blade
and misericordia

Vexilus Praetor with storm shield
and misericordia

Custodian Guard with sentinel blade,
storm shield and misericordia

Custodian Warden with guardian spear
and misericordia

Shield-Captain with guardian spear
and misericordia

Custodian Warden with guardian spear
and misericordia

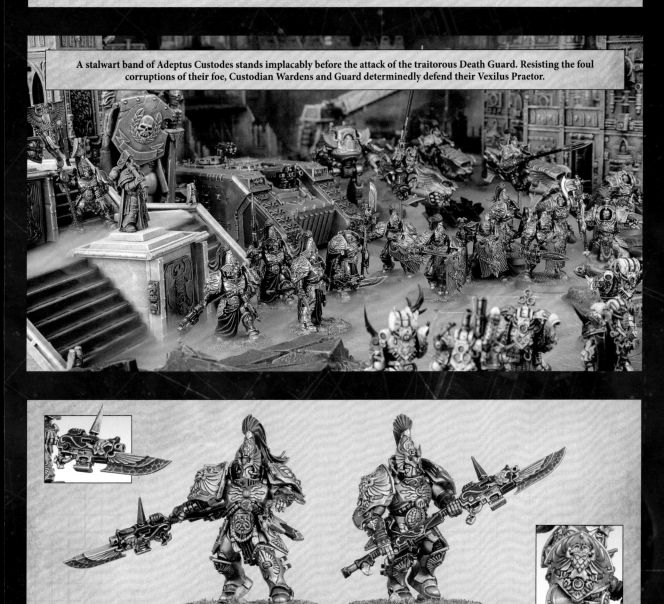

A stalwart band of Adeptus Custodes stands implacably before the attack of the traitorous Death Guard. Resisting the foul corruptions of their foe, Custodian Wardens and Guard determinedly defend their Vexilus Praetor.

Custodian Guard with guardian spears and misericordia

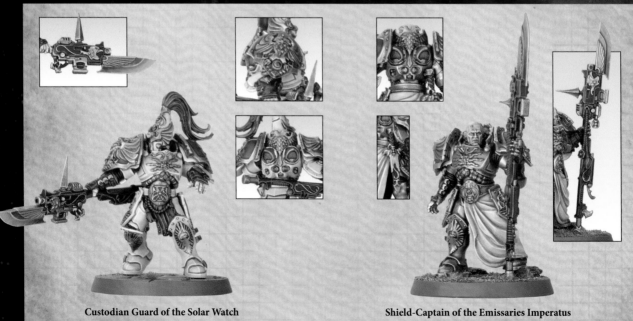

Custodian Guard of the Solar Watch

Shield-Captain of the Emissaries Imperatus

Amidst the frozen northern reaches of Gathalamor Prime, a proud force of the Adeptus Custodes bear the brunt of the Black Legion charge, steadying the line while the Astra Militarum bring up heavy armour to bombard the Chaos forces.

Allarus Custodian of the Dread Host

Custodian Guard of the Shadowkeepers

Vastly outnumbered by wave upon wave of Bad Moons Orks, an elite band of Custodians hold their ground, defending the bunker complex of the Tyborial astropathic choir.

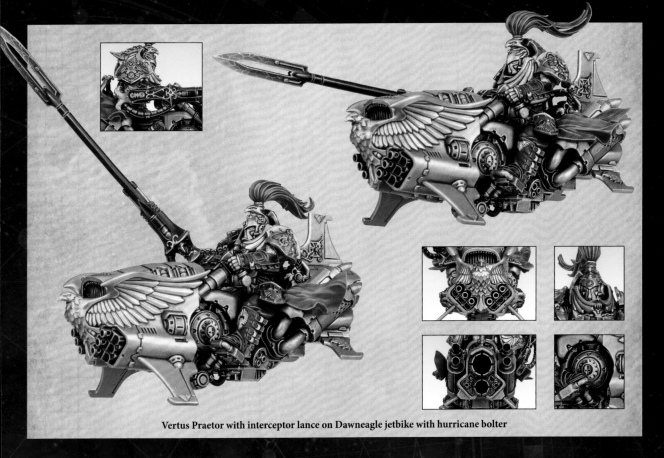

Vertus Praetor with interceptor lance on Dawneagle jetbike with hurricane bolter

A squadron of Vertus Praetors skims low through the ecclesiastical ruins of Glorificum Alpha, their auspicators hunting for armoured targets to bring low.

Allarus Custodians with castellan axes, balistus grenade launchers and misericordia

Vexilus Praetor in Allarus
Terminator armour

Allarus Custodian with guardian spear
and balistus grenade launcher

A pair of Venerable Contemptor Dreadnoughts stomp forwards at the head of the Adeptus Custodes advance, one firing its Kheres-pattern assault cannon while the other blasts the enemy with the superheated energies of its multi-melta.

THE EAGLE VIGILANS

The Adeptus Custodes have access to a selection of the most powerful characters, units and war engines in the Warhammer 40,000 universe. With every model a champion in its own right, there are countless ways in which armies of Custodians can be built. This section provides inspiration for your own collection by showing a few examples.

With just six models in total, the force below may look small. Yet so powerful is every warrior in this collection that it can go toe to toe with tabletop armies several times its size from any of the other Warhammer 40,000 factions. Even better, this force can be built from the contents of just two boxes of miniatures – the Custodian Guard Squad box and the Contemptor Dreadnought box – and its comparatively low model count means that you can lavish time and attention

upon every single one of your Adeptus Custodes miniatures.

This collection is a good example of a small shield company. It is led by Shield-Captain Nathadian Steale, who wields a sentinel blade with deadly effect while deflecting his enemy's blades and blasts with a mighty storm shield. At Steale's side stands Caltor Tasolian, a veteran of dozens of war zones and the shield company's Vexilus Praetor.

Heavy firepower and armoured strength is provided by a Venerable Contemptor Dreadnought, Eratorius. Meanwhile, the force's mainstay warriors are a squad of Custodian Guard who refer to themselves as the Protectors of the Throne.

As well as being a great starting force, this collection fulfils the requirements of a Patrol Detachment, providing you with three command points for being Battle-forged to spend on vital Stratagems.

Captain Nathadian Steale leads his shield company, the Eagle Vigilans, into battle.

FURY OF TERRA SHIELD HOST

Once a collection of Warhammer 40,000 Citadel Miniatures is started, it inevitably grows into a sizeable battlefield force. This shield host, led by Captain-General Trajann Valoris and boasting two sizeable shield companies amongst its ranks, is an excellent example of how an Adeptus Custodes collection can become a truly impressive tabletop army.

The Fury of Terra shield host was assembled by Trajann Valoris to meet the threat of a massive Heretic Astartes assault against Elysia. This collection is built around the starting force detailed on the previous page, and fulfils the requirements of both a Battalion and a Vanguard Detachment, each of which can be considered a shield company. This provides the player with an impressive seven command points to spend on their Stratagems!

The first of these Detachments, the Battalion, is led by none other than the Captain-General himself. Though a renowned warrior, Valoris is wise enough to know that even he requires counsel

in the heat of battle. Thus the battalion also includes Shield-Captain Anatolyn Ganorth, who is expected to both act as Valoris' naysmith and fight valiantly at his right hand. Vexilus Praetor Toxvyrd Basillaeus carries the shield company's vexilla into battle, completing the command elements of his force.

Meanwhile, its auramite core consists of three units of Custodian Guard. These warriors, the Protectors of the Throne, the Watchmen and the Auric Blades, are each capable of overcoming enemies many times their own number. Between them they form a force that can go blade-to-blade with any foe in the galaxy.

The remainder of the Battalion comprises Contemptor Dreadnought Darian, and the Allarus Custodians known as the Solar Lions. This latter force rides to battle aboard the accomplished Venerable Land Raider *Wrath of Ages*, and can single-handedly shatter an enemy's battle line.

The second shield company, the Vanguard Detachment, is somewhat more esoteric in its composition. Led by Shield-Captain Steale and his comrade Vexilus Praetor Tasolian, the force is almost solely comprised of units with the Elites battlefield role. Two stalwart bands of Custodian Wardens, the Indomitors and the Emperor's Sentinels, form its immovable centre and ensure that this shield host can seize crucial battlefield locations and deny them to even the most aggressive enemy attacks. Another Dreadnought, Eratorius, marches alongside the Wardens. Meanwhile, providing the force with a high-speed, hard-hitting element, the Vertus Praetors known as Sol's Arrows streak ahead to scout out and annihilate threats.

1. Captain-General
   Trajann Valoris

2. Shield-Captain Ganorth

3. Shield-Captain Steale

4. Vexilus Praetor Tasolian

5. Vexilus Praetor Basillaeus

6. Custodian Guard,
   The Protectors of the Throne

7. Custodian Guard,
   The Watchmen

8. Custodian Guard,
   The Auric Blades

9. Allarus Custodians,
   The Solar Lions

10. Custodian Wardens,
    The Emperor's Sentinels

11. Custodian Wardens,
    The Indomitors

12. Venerable Contemptor
    Dreadnought, Eratorius

13. Venerable Contemptor
    Dreadnought, Darian

14. Vertus Praetors, Sol's Arrows

15. Venerable Land Raider,
    Wrath of Ages

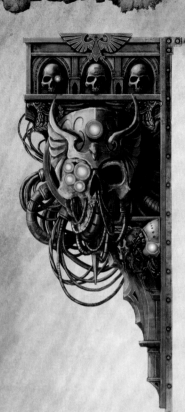

THE ARMY OF TERRA

This section contains all of the datasheets that you will need to fight battles with your Adeptus Custodes miniatures, and the rules for the weapons they can wield in battle. Each datasheet includes the characteristics profiles of the unit it describes, as well as any weapons and special abilities it may have. Any abilities that are common to several units are described below and referenced on the datasheets themselves.

ABILITIES

The following ability is common to all **ADEPTUS CUSTODES** units.

AEGIS OF THE EMPEROR

The cellular alchemy that creates the warriors of the Adeptus Custodes leaves them forever touched by a spark of the Emperor's own greatness. Beyond their martial might and incorruptible nobility, this energy manifests itself as an almost supernatural warding, as though the Custodians were protected by the hand of the Emperor. Bullets and bolts are turned aside at the last moment, blades fail to strike home, and even the psychic powers of the foe can suddenly and inexplicably flicker away to nothing in the face of the Ten Thousand.

Models with this ability have a 5+ invulnerable save.

In addition, roll a D6 each time a model with this ability suffers a mortal wound in the Psychic phase. On a 6 that mortal wound is ignored.

'Rare is the battle where the Emperor's Custodians outnumber our foes. We are ever beset, surrounded upon all sides by heresy and foulness just as is Terra itself. Yet like the throneworld we stand resolute, indefatigable, indomitable. Let the enemy come, let them darken the horizon with their numbers. Still we will prevail.'

- *Allarus Custodian Harkhas Bastoris*

A shield company of the Adeptus Custodes advance through the ruins of Vostagraad, blades at the ready and weapons primed to annihilate the heretic foe before they can endanger the throneworld.

CAPTAIN-GENERAL TRAJANN VALORIS

NAME	M	WS	BS	S	T	W	A	Ld	Sv
Captain-General Trajann Valoris	6"	2+	2+	5	5	7	5	10	2+

Captain-General Trajann Valoris is a single model armed with the Watcher's Axe and a misericordia. Only one of this model may be included in your army.

WEAPON	RANGE	TYPE	S	AP	D	ABILITIES
Watcher's Axe (shooting)	24"	Rapid Fire 1	5	-1	2	-
Misericordia	Melee	Melee	User	-2	1	Each time the bearer fights, it can make 1 additional attack with this weapon unless it is also equipped with a storm shield.
Watcher's Axe (melee)	Melee	Melee	x2	-3	D3	-

ABILITIES	
Aegis of the Emperor (pg 56) **Auramite Halo:** Trajann Valoris has a 3+ invulnerable save. **Legendary Commander:** You can re-roll hit rolls and wound rolls of 1 made for friendly **ADEPTUS CUSTODES** units within 6" of Trajann Valoris.	**Moment Shackle:** Once per battle, if Trajann Valoris is on the battlefield, you can do one of the following: • Regain D3 wounds lost by Trajann Valoris during this phase (you cannot do this during an attack or if Trajann Valoris is slain). • At the end of the Fight phase, pile in and attack with Trajann Valoris an additional time. • Regain up to D3 Command Points spent when you use a Stratagem (but no more than were spent on the Stratagem).

FACTION KEYWORDS	IMPERIUM, ADEPTUS CUSTODES

KEYWORDS	CHARACTER, INFANTRY, CAPTAIN-GENERAL TRAJANN VALORIS

'The hotter the forge, the finer the blade, or so they say. The forge of war in which we now find ourselves blazes hotter than anything the Imperium has seen in ten millennia. We of the Adeptus Custodes were built to endure these fires. They will not be our end. Instead, we will be honed to the finest cutting edge, that we may be the bane of even the foulest heretics.'

- Captain-General Trajann Valoris

> 'We are vigilance unending. We are duty unstinting. We are punishment inescapable. We are the Adeptus Custodes, and all must fear our wrath.'
> - *Shield-Captain Rothrian Ganyth*

A Shield-Captain holds his guardian spear and his misericordia ready as he leads his comrades to war.

SHIELD-CAPTAIN

NAME	M	WS	BS	S	T	W	A	Ld	Sv
Shield-Captain	6"	2+	2+	5	5	6	5	9	2+

A Shield-Captain is a single model armed with a guardian spear.

WEAPON	RANGE	TYPE	S	AP	D	ABILITIES
Castellan axe (shooting)	24"	Rapid Fire 1	4	-1	2	-
Guardian spear (shooting)	24"	Rapid Fire 1	4	-1	2	-
Sentinel blade (shooting)	12"	Pistol 2	4	0	1	-
Castellan axe (melee)	Melee	Melee	+3	-2	D3	-
Guardian spear (melee)	Melee	Melee	+1	-3	D3	-
Misericordia	Melee	Melee	User	-2	1	Each time the bearer fights, it can make 1 additional attack with this weapon unless it is also equipped with a storm shield.
Sentinel blade (melee)	Melee	Melee	User	-3	D3	-

WARGEAR OPTIONS	• This model may replace its guardian spear with a sentinel blade or a castellan axe. • This model may take a misericordia. • If this model is armed with a sentinel blade, it may take a storm shield.

ABILITIES	**Aegis of the Emperor** (pg 56) **Inspirational Fighter:** You can re-roll hit rolls of 1 made for friendly **ADEPTUS CUSTODES** units within 6" of this model.	**Storm Shield:** A model equipped with a storm shield has a 3+ invulnerable save.

FACTION KEYWORDS	**IMPERIUM, ADEPTUS CUSTODES**
KEYWORDS	**CHARACTER, INFANTRY, SHIELD-CAPTAIN**

SHIELD-CAPTAIN
in Allarus Terminator Armour

8 POWER

NAME	M	WS	BS	S	T	W	A	Ld	Sv
Shield-Captain in Allarus Terminator Armour	6"	2+	2+	5	5	7	5	9	2+

A Shield-Captain in Allarus Terminator Armour is a single model armed with a guardian spear and balistus grenade launcher.

WEAPON	RANGE	TYPE	S	AP	D	ABILITIES
Balistus grenade launcher	12"	Assault D3	4	-3	1	-
Castellan axe (shooting)	24"	Rapid Fire 1	4	-1	2	-
Guardian spear (shooting)	24"	Rapid Fire 1	4	-1	2	-
Castellan axe (melee)	Melee	Melee	+3	-2	D3	-
Guardian spear (melee)	Melee	Melee	+1	-3	D3	-
Misericordia	Melee	Melee	User	-2	1	Each time the bearer fights, it can make 1 additional attack with this weapon unless it is also equipped with a storm shield.

WARGEAR OPTIONS	• This model may replace its guardian spear with a castellan axe. • This model may take a misericordia.

ABILITIES	**Aegis of the Emperor** (pg 56) **Inspirational Fighter:** You can re-roll hit rolls of 1 made for friendly **Adeptus Custodes** units within 6" of this model.	**From Golden Light:** During deployment, you can set up this model in a Godstrike-pattern teleportarium array instead of placing it on the battlefield. At the end of any of your Movement phases this model can teleport into battle – set it up anywhere on the battlefield that is more than 9" away from any enemy models.

FACTION KEYWORDS	**Imperium, Adeptus Custodes**
KEYWORDS	**Character, Infantry, Terminator, Shield-Captain**

SHIELD-CAPTAIN
on Dawneagle Jetbike

9 POWER

NAME	M	WS	BS	S	T	W	A	Ld	Sv
Shield-Captain on Dawneagle Jetbike	14"	2+	2+	5	6	7	5	9	2+

A Shield-Captain on Dawneagle Jetbike is a single model armed with an interceptor lance. His jetbike is equipped with a hurricane bolter.

WEAPON	RANGE	TYPE	S	AP	D	ABILITIES
Hurricane bolter	24"	Rapid Fire 6	4	0	1	-
Salvo launcher	When attacking with this weapon, choose one of the profiles below.					
- Melta missile	24"	Heavy 1	8	-4	D6	You can re-roll failed wound rolls for this weapon if the target is a **Vehicle**.
- Flakkburst missile	24"	Heavy D3	7	-1	D3	Add 1 to all hit rolls made for this weapon against targets that can **Fly**. Subtract 1 from the hit rolls made for this weapon against all other targets.
Interceptor lance	Melee	Melee	+1	-3	D3	You can re-roll failed wound rolls for this weapon on a turn in which its bearer made a successful charge.
Misericordia	Melee	Melee	User	-2	1	Each time the bearer fights, it can make 1 additional attack with this weapon unless it is also equipped with a storm shield.

WARGEAR OPTIONS	• This model may replace its hurricane bolter with a salvo launcher. • This model may take a misericordia.

ABILITIES	**Aegis of the Emperor** (pg 56) **Inspirational Fighter:** You can re-roll hit rolls of 1 made for friendly **Adeptus Custodes** units within 6" of this model.	**Implacable Vanguard:** When this model Advances, add 6" to its Move characteristic for that Movement phase instead of rolling a dice.

FACTION KEYWORDS	**Imperium, Adeptus Custodes**
KEYWORDS	**Character, Biker, Fly, Shield-Captain**

CUSTODIAN GUARD

NAME	M	WS	BS	S	T	W	A	Ld	Sv
Custodian Guard	6"	2+	2+	5	5	3	3	8	2+

This unit contains 3 Custodian Guard. It can include up to 7 additional Custodian Guard (**Power Rating +3 per model**). Each model is armed with a guardian spear.

WEAPON	RANGE	TYPE	S	AP	D	ABILITIES
Guardian spear (shooting)	24"	Rapid Fire 1	4	-1	2	-
Sentinel blade (shooting)	12"	Pistol 2	4	0	1	-
Guardian spear (melee)	Melee	Melee	+1	-3	D3	-
Misericordia	Melee	Melee	User	-2	1	Each time the bearer fights, it can make 1 additional attack with this weapon unless it is also equipped with a storm shield.
Sentinel blade (melee)	Melee	Melee	User	-3	D3	-

WARGEAR OPTIONS	• Any model may replace its guardian spear with a sentinel blade and storm shield. • Any model may take a misericordia.
ABILITIES	**Aegis of the Emperor** (pg 56) **Storm Shield:** A model equipped with a storm shield has a 3+ invulnerable save.
FACTION KEYWORDS	IMPERIUM, ADEPTUS CUSTODES
KEYWORDS	INFANTRY, CUSTODIAN GUARD

Storming from the sanctum gates with their bolt weapons blazing, the Custodian Guard drive the Thousand Sons back.

CUSTODIAN WARDENS

NAME	M	WS	BS	S	T	W	A	Ld	Sv
Custodian Warden	6"	2+	2+	5	5	3	4	9	2+

This unit contains 3 Custodian Wardens. It can include up to 7 additional Custodian Wardens (**Power Rating +4 per model**). Each model is armed with a castellan axe and misericordia.

WEAPON	RANGE	TYPE	S	AP	D	ABILITIES
Castellan axe (shooting)	24"	Rapid Fire 1	4	-1	2	-
Guardian spear (shooting)	24"	Rapid Fire 1	4	-1	2	-
Castellan axe (melee)	Melee	Melee	+3	-2	D3	-
Guardian spear (melee)	Melee	Melee	+1	-3	D3	-
Misericordia	Melee	Melee	User	-2	1	Each time the bearer fights, it can make 1 additional attack with this weapon unless it is also equipped with a storm shield.

WARGEAR OPTIONS	• Any model may replace its castellan axe with a guardian spear.
ABILITIES	**Aegis of the Emperor** (pg 56) **Binding Oaths:** Roll a D6 each time a model in this unit loses a wound; on a 6 the damage is ignored and that wound is not lost.
FACTION KEYWORDS	**IMPERIUM, ADEPTUS CUSTODES**
KEYWORDS	**INFANTRY, CUSTODIAN WARDENS**

Custodian Wardens stand firm against the advancing Chaos Space Marine forces.

'Raise your vexilla high! Though the battlefield might
blaze with the fury of the foe, though death might whirl
about you in a storm, though the fallen may lie ten deep
underfoot, raise your vexilla! Drive back the darkness
and horror with its golden radiance, until all is redeemed
by the glory of the Emperor of Mankind.'

– Aetheus Urdanesh, Vexilus Praetor

VEXILUS PRAETOR
IN ALLARUS TERMINATOR ARMOUR

7 POWER

NAME	M	WS	BS	S	T	W	A	Ld	Sv
Vexilus Praetor in Allarus Terminator Armour	6"	2+	2+	5	5	6	4	9	2+

A Vexilus Praetor in Allarus Terminator Armour is a single model armed with a balistus grenade launcher.

WEAPON	RANGE	TYPE	S	AP	D	ABILITIES
Balistus grenade launcher	12"	Assault D3	4	-3	1	-
Misericordia	Melee	Melee	User	-2	1	Each time the bearer fights, it can make 1 additional attack with this weapon unless it is also equipped with a storm shield.

WARGEAR OPTIONS	• This model may take a misericordia.

ABILITIES	**Aegis of the Emperor** (pg 56)

From Golden Light: During deployment, you can set up this model in a Godstrike-pattern teleportarium array instead of placing it on the battlefield. At the end of any of your Movement phases this model can teleport into battle – set it up anywhere on the battlefield that is more than 9" away from any enemy models.

Custodes Vexilla: You can re-roll failed Morale tests for friendly **IMPERIUM INFANTRY** and **BIKER** units within 6" of this model. In addition, when you add this model to your army, choose one of the following vexillas for this model to carry:

• Vexilla Imperius: **ADEPTUS CUSTODES** models (other than **VEHICLES**) add 1 to their Attacks characteristic whilst their unit is within 6" of any friendly **VEXILUS PRAETORS** with this vexilla.

• Vexilla Defensor: **IMPERIUM INFANTRY** units have a 5+ invulnerable save against ranged weapons whilst they are wholly within 9" of any friendly **VEXILUS PRAETORS** with this vexilla.

• Vexilla Magnifica: Your opponent must subtract 1 from hit rolls in the Shooting phase for attacks that target **ADEPTUS CUSTODES** units within 6" of any friendly **VEXILUS PRAETORS** with this vexilla.

FACTION KEYWORDS	**IMPERIUM, ADEPTUS CUSTODES**
KEYWORDS	**CHARACTER, INFANTRY, TERMINATOR, VEXILUS PRAETOR**

VEXILUS PRAETOR

6 POWER

NAME	M	WS	BS	S	T	W	A	Ld	Sv
Vexilus Praetor	6"	2+	2+	5	5	5	4	9	2+

A Vexilus Praetor is a single model armed with a guardian spear, castellan axe or storm shield.

WEAPON	RANGE	TYPE	S	AP	D	ABILITIES
Castellan axe (shooting)	24"	Rapid Fire 1	4	-1	2	-
Guardian spear (shooting)	24"	Rapid Fire 1	4	-1	2	-
Castellan axe (melee)	Melee	Melee	+3	-2	D3	-
Guardian spear (melee)	Melee	Melee	+1	-3	D3	-
Misericordia	Melee	Melee	User	-2	1	Each time the bearer fights, it can make 1 additional attack with this weapon unless it is also equipped with a storm shield.

WARGEAR OPTIONS
- This model may replace its guardian spear, castellan axe or storm shield with a misericordia.
- If this model does not replace its wargear with a misericordia, it may take a misericordia.

ABILITIES

Aegis of the Emperor (pg 56)

Storm Shield: A model equipped with a storm shield has a 3+ invulnerable save.

Custodes Vexilla: You can re-roll failed Morale tests for friendly **IMPERIUM INFANTRY** and **BIKER** units within 6" of this model. In addition, when you add this model to your army, choose one of the following vexillas for this model to carry:

- **Vexilla Imperius:** **ADEPTUS CUSTODES** models (other than **VEHICLES**) add 1 to their Attacks characteristic whilst their unit is within 6" of any friendly **VEXILUS PRAETORS** with this vexilla.

- **Vexilla Defensor:** **IMPERIUM INFANTRY** units have a 5+ invulnerable save against ranged weapons whilst they are wholly within 9" of any friendly **VEXILUS PRAETORS** with this vexilla.

- **Vexilla Magnifica:** Your opponent must subtract 1 from hit rolls in the Shooting phase for attacks that target **ADEPTUS CUSTODES** units within 6" of any friendly **VEXILUS PRAETORS** with this vexilla.

FACTION KEYWORDS | **IMPERIUM, ADEPTUS CUSTODES**

KEYWORDS | **CHARACTER, INFANTRY, VEXILUS PRAETOR**

'IT WAS UPON GATHALAMOR PRIME, BEFORE THE RUINS OF THE SANCTIC CITADEL, THAT CUSTODIAN ERASMIAN ALHORIS CASSABAR LYCHANSIS SLEW A TRIO OF TRAITOR CHAMPIONS SINGLE-HANDED. THOUGH BLOODIED BY THE FIGHT NEAR-UNTO DEATH, LYCHANSIS BATTLED ON FOR SIX MORE HOURS AND FELLED DOZENS OF THE HERETIC FOE. AT BATTLE'S END, WHEN THE THREAT WAS PASSED AND HIS WOUNDS BOUND, LYCHANSIS' COMRADES AGREED THAT HE HAD EARNED GREAT HONOUR THROUGH HIS DEEDS. SO DID HE BECOME A VEXILUS PRAETOR, WHO WOULD BEAR HIS SHIELD COMPANY'S HONOUR ONTO THE FIELD OF WAR.'

- Extract, the Battle for Gathalamor

ALLARUS CUSTODIANS

NAME	M	WS	BS	S	T	W	A	Ld	Sv
Allarus Custodian	6"	2+	2+	5	5	4	4	9	2+

This unit contains 3 Allarus Custodians. It can include up to 7 additional Allarus Custodians (**Power Rating +5 per model**). Each model is armed with a castellan axe and a balistus grenade launcher.

WEAPON	RANGE	TYPE	S	AP	D	ABILITIES
Balistus grenade launcher	12"	Assault D3	4	-3	1	-
Castellan axe (shooting)	24"	Rapid Fire 1	4	-1	2	-
Guardian spear (shooting)	24"	Rapid Fire 1	4	-1	2	-
Castellan axe (melee)	Melee	Melee	+3	-2	D3	-
Guardian spear (melee)	Melee	Melee	+1	-3	D3	-
Misericordia	Melee	Melee	User	-2	1	Each time the bearer fights, it can make 1 additional attack with this weapon unless it is also equipped with a storm shield.

WARGEAR OPTIONS	• Any model may replace its castellan axe with a guardian spear. • Any model may take a misericordia.	
ABILITIES	**Aegis of the Emperor** (pg 56) **Slayers of Tyrants:** When models in this unit pile in and consolidate, they can move up to 3" towards the nearest enemy **CHARACTER** even if it is not the nearest enemy model, so long as they finish this move within 1" of an enemy unit.	**From Golden Light:** During deployment, you can set up this unit in a Godstrike-pattern teleportarium array instead of placing them on the battlefield. At the end of any of your Movement phases they can teleport into battle – set them up anywhere on the battlefield that is more than 9" away from any enemy models.
FACTION KEYWORDS	**IMPERIUM, ADEPTUS CUSTODES**	
KEYWORDS	**INFANTRY, TERMINATOR, ALLARUS CUSTODIANS**	

As the teleport flare subsides, a trio of Allarus Custodians step forth to lock blades with the putrescent Death Guard.

10 POWER

VENERABLE CONTEMPTOR DREADNOUGHT

DAMAGE

Some of this model's characteristics change as it suffers damage, as shown below:

NAME	M	WS	BS	S	T	W	A	Ld	Sv
Venerable Contemptor Dreadnought	*	*	*	7	7	10	4	8	2+

REMAINING W	M	WS	BS
6-10+	9"	2+	2+
3-5	6"	3+	3+
1-2	4"	4+	4+

A Venerable Contemptor Dreadnought is a single model equipped with a Dreadnought combat weapon, multi-melta and combi-bolter.

WEAPON	RANGE	TYPE	S	AP	D	ABILITIES
Combi-bolter	24"	Rapid Fire 2	4	0	1	-
Kheres-pattern assault cannon	24"	Heavy 6	7	-1	1	-
Multi-melta	24"	Heavy 1	8	-4	D6	If the target is within half range of this weapon, roll two dice when inflicting damage with it and discard the lowest result.
Dreadnought combat weapon	Melee	Melee	x2	-3	3	-

WARGEAR OPTIONS	• This model may replace its multi-melta with a Kheres-pattern assault cannon.

ABILITIES	**Atomantic Shielding:** This model has a 5+ invulnerable save. **Unyielding Ancient:** Roll a D6 each time this model loses a wound; on a 6 the damage is ignored and that wound is not lost.	**Explodes:** If this model is reduced to 0 wounds, roll a D6 before removing it from the battlefield. On a 6 it explodes, and each unit within 6" suffers D3 mortal wounds.

FACTION KEYWORDS	IMPERIUM, ADEPTUS CUSTODES

KEYWORDS	VEHICLE, DREADNOUGHT, VENERABLE CONTEMPTOR DREADNOUGHT

'I fought atop the walls of the Emperor's palace when the Great Beast's Waaagh! crashed against them. There I fell, yet was reborn in this ageless body of auramite. I fought upon the battlefields of Ghosaris during the Moirae Schism, and crushed the servants of the Dark Mechanicus without mercy. I stood immovable in the face of the Blood Cults of Tsydon, and slew all who came against me. Still I fight, and so shall I always, for my debt to the Emperor shall never be paid.'

- Venerable Contemptor Dreadnought Uriaxes

Streaking down from the lofty heights of the Spire of Victories, the Vertus Praetors swoop into battle.

VERTUS PRAETORS

NAME	M	WS	BS	S	T	W	A	Ld	Sv
Vertus Praetor	14"	2+	2+	5	6	4	4	9	2+

This unit contains 3 Vertus Praetors. It can include up to 7 additional Vertus Praetors (**Power Rating +5 per model**). Each model is armed with an interceptor lance, and each of their Dawneagle jetbikes is equipped with a hurricane bolter.

WEAPON	RANGE	TYPE	S	AP	D	ABILITIES
Hurricane bolter	24"	Rapid Fire 6	4	0	1	-
Salvo launcher	When attacking with this weapon, choose one of the profiles below.					
- Melta missile	24"	Heavy 1	8	-4	D6	You can re-roll failed wound rolls for this weapon if the target is a **VEHICLE**.
- Flakkburst missile	24"	Heavy D3	7	-1	D3	Add 1 to all hit rolls made for this weapon against targets that can **FLY**. Subtract 1 from the hit rolls made for this weapon against all other targets.
Interceptor lance	Melee	Melee	+1	-3	D3	You can re-roll failed wound rolls for this weapon on a turn in which its bearer made a successful charge.
Misericordia	Melee	Melee	User	-2	1	Each time the bearer fights, it can make 1 additional attack with this weapon unless it is also equipped with a storm shield.

WARGEAR OPTIONS	• Any model may replace its hurricane bolter with a salvo launcher. • Any model may take a misericordia.
ABILITIES	**Aegis of the Emperor** (pg 56) **Implacable Vanguard:** When this unit Advances, add 6" to its Move characteristic for that Movement phase instead of rolling a dice.
FACTION KEYWORDS	**IMPERIUM, ADEPTUS CUSTODES**
KEYWORDS	**BIKER, FLY, VERTUS PRAETORS**

VENERABLE LAND RAIDER

NAME	M	WS	BS	S	T	W	A	Ld	Sv
Venerable Land Raider	*	6+	*	8	8	16	*	9	2+

DAMAGE

Some of this model's characteristics change as it suffers damage, as shown below:

REMAINING W	M	BS	A
9-16+	10"	2+	6
5-8	5"	3+	D6
1-4	3"	4+	1

A Venerable Land Raider is a single model equipped with a twin heavy bolter and two twin lascannons.

WEAPON	RANGE	TYPE	S	AP	D	ABILITIES
Hunter-killer missile	48"	Heavy 1	8	-2	D6	A model can only fire each of its hunter-killer missiles once per battle.
Storm bolter	24"	Rapid Fire 2	4	0	1	-
Twin heavy bolter	36"	Heavy 6	5	-1	1	-
Twin lascannon	48"	Heavy 2	9	-3	D6	-

WARGEAR OPTIONS	• This model may take a hunter-killer missile. • This model may take a storm bolter.

ABILITIES	**Power of the Machine Spirit:** This model does not suffer the penalty to hit rolls for moving and firing Heavy weapons. **Smoke Launchers:** Once per game, instead of shooting any weapons in the Shooting phase, this model can use its smoke launchers; until your next Shooting phase your opponent must subtract 1 from all hit rolls for ranged weapons that target this vehicle.	**Unyielding Ancient:** Roll a D6 each time this model loses a wound; on a 6 the damage is ignored and that wound is not lost. **Explodes:** If this model is reduced to 0 wounds, roll a D6 before removing it from the battlefield and before any embarked models disembark. On a 6 it explodes, and each unit within 6" suffers D6 mortal wounds.

TRANSPORT	This model can transport 5 **ADEPTUS CUSTODES INFANTRY** models.

FACTION KEYWORDS	**IMPERIUM, ADEPTUS CUSTODES**

KEYWORDS	**VEHICLE, TRANSPORT, LAND RAIDER, VENERABLE LAND RAIDER**

A Venerable Land Raider rumbles through the fog shrouded streets, weapons tracking in search of targets.

ARMOURY OF THE ADEPTUS CUSTODES

The Adeptus Custodes have weapons and wargear unparalleled across the galaxy, each a masterwork of absolute lethality in the hands of the Emperor's guardians. The profiles for all of their wargear are detailed below.

RANGED WEAPONS

WEAPON	RANGE	TYPE	S	AP	D	ABILITIES
Balistus grenade launcher	12"	Assault D3	4	-3	1	-
Castellan axe (shooting)	24"	Rapid Fire 1	4	-1	2	-
Combi-bolter	24"	Rapid Fire 2	4	0	1	-
Guardian spear (shooting)	24"	Rapid Fire 1	4	-1	2	-
Hunter-killer missile	48"	Heavy 1	8	-2	D6	A model can only fire each of its hunter-killer missiles once per battle.
Hurricane bolter	24"	Rapid Fire 6	4	0	1	-
Kheres-pattern assault cannon	24"	Heavy 6	7	-1	1	-
Multi-melta	24"	Heavy 1	8	-4	D6	If the target is within half range of this weapon, roll two dice when inflicting damage with it and discard the lowest result.
Salvo launcher	When attacking with this weapon, choose one of the profiles below.					
- Melta missile	24"	Heavy 1	8	-4	D6	You can re-roll failed wound rolls for this weapon if the target is a **Vehicle**.
- Flakkburst missile	24"	Heavy D3	7	-1	D3	Add 1 to all hit rolls made for this weapon against targets that can **Fly**. Subtract 1 from the hit rolls made for this weapon against all other targets.
Sentinel blade (shooting)	12"	Pistol 2	4	0	1	-
Storm bolter	24"	Rapid Fire 2	4	0	1	-
Twin heavy bolter	36"	Heavy 6	5	-1	1	-
Twin lascannon	48"	Heavy 2	9	-3	D6	-
Watcher's Axe (shooting)	24"	Rapid Fire 1	5	-1	2	-

MELEE WEAPONS

WEAPON	RANGE	TYPE	S	AP	D	ABILITIES
Castellan axe (melee)	Melee	Melee	+3	-2	D3	-
Dreadnought combat weapon	Melee	Melee	x2	-3	3	-
Guardian spear (melee)	Melee	Melee	+1	-3	D3	-
Interceptor lance	Melee	Melee	+1	-3	D3	You can re-roll failed wound rolls for this weapon on a turn in which its bearer made a successful charge.
Misericordia	Melee	Melee	User	-2	1	Each time the bearer fights, it can make 1 additional attack with this weapon unless it is also equipped with a storm shield.
Sentinel blade (melee)	Melee	Melee	User	-3	D3	-
Watcher's Axe (melee)	Melee	Melee	x2	-3	D3	-

'When all other recourse is deemed insufficient, when the throneworld itself stands square in the path of peril, then are the Adeptus Custodes unleashed. For such crucial theatres of war, where defeat could bring the ruin of Mankind itself, it is our solemn duty to provide these heroes with the very finest weapons and armour that Humanity can provide. To do any less would be foolish, dishonourable and tantamount to heresy of the highest order.'

- Nurthias Drund, Master Artificer of the Forge Aquilan

As the Great Rift burst open like a ragged wound, the Blood Legions of Khorne spilled forth to attack Holy Terra itself. Stood upon the steps before the Lion's Gate, Trajann Valoris and Roboute Guilliman led the combined force that drove them back.

AURIC MORTALIS

In this section you'll find rules for Battle-forged armies that include ADEPTUS CUSTODES Detachments – that is, any Detachment which only includes ADEPTUS CUSTODES units. These rules include the abilities below and a series of Stratagems. This section also includes the Adeptus Custodes' unique Warlord Traits, Relics and Tactical Objectives. Together, these rules reflect the character and fighting style of the Adeptus Custodes in your games of Warhammer 40,000.

ABILITIES

If your army is Battle-forged, all INFANTRY and BIKER units in ADEPTUS CUSTODES Detachments gain the Sworn Guardians and the Emperor's Chosen abilities.

THE EMPEROR'S CHOSEN

The foremost guardians of the Emperor are eternally blessed, bearing the Master of Mankind's unearthly protection at all times.

This unit's invulnerable save is improved by 1 (to a maximum of 3+).

SWORN GUARDIANS

The Ten Thousand are the ultimate executors of the Emperor's will. They fight with absolute certainty and an unshakeable conviction in the rightness and necessity of their every action. They possess a truly manifest destiny, and they are as unstoppable in seizing that which is theirs – and by extension the Emperor's – as they are in defending it.

A unit with this ability that is within range of an objective marker (as specified in the mission) controls the objective marker even if there are more enemy models within range of that objective marker. If an enemy unit within range of the same objective marker has a similar ability, then the objective marker is controlled by the player who has the most models within range of it as normal.

'The Emperor's realm is a festering ruin of overcrowded worlds drowning in their own ignorance and fear. It is a tumbledown ghetto that burns from end to end with the flames of war. They do not deserve their Emperor. They do not deserve us. None of that alters the fact that our duty must be done…'

- Telchor, Custodian Guard

STRATAGEMS

If your army is Battle-forged and includes any ADEPTUS CUSTODES Detachments (excluding Auxiliary Support Detachments), you have access to the Stratagems shown on the following pages, meaning you can spend Command Points to activate them. These reflect the unique strategies used by the forces of the Adeptus Custodes on the battlefield.

1CP/3CP — FROM GOLDEN LIGHT THEY COME
Adeptus Custodes Stratagem

Through use of ancient Godstrike-pattern teleportariums, the Custodians can deploy straight into the heart of battle.

Use this Stratagem during deployment. Instead of placing them on the battlefield, you can set up one ADEPTUS CUSTODES INFANTRY, BIKER or DREADNOUGHT unit from your army in a Godstrike-pattern teleportarium array for 1 CP, or two such units for 3 CPs. At the end of any of your Movement phases these units can teleport into battle – set them up anywhere on the battlefield that is more than 9" away from any enemy models. This Stratagem can only be used once per battle.

1CP — UNFLINCHING
Adeptus Custodes Stratagem

With glacial calm and superhuman reactions, the Custodians meet the enemy charge with a hail of deadly firepower.

Use this Stratagem in your opponent's Charge phase. Choose an ADEPTUS CUSTODES unit from your army. When models in this unit fire Overwatch in this phase, they require a roll of 5+ (rather than 6) to successfully hit.

2CP — UNLEASH THE LIONS
Adeptus Custodes Stratagem

Many are the tales of heroic bands of Allarus Custodians engaging entire armies in fierce battle.

Use this Stratagem at the start of your Movement phase. Select a unit of Allarus Custodians from your army on the battlefield. That unit is immediately split into separate units, each containing a single model.

1CP — TANGLEFOOT GRENADE
Adeptus Custodes Stratagem

These rare grenades cause localised distortions in gravity, space and time that send the enemy stumbling in disarray.

Use this Stratagem at the beginning of your opponent's Movement or Charge phase. Choose an enemy unit within 12" of an ADEPTUS CUSTODES INFANTRY unit from your army and roll a D6. Your opponent must reduce that unit's Movement characteristic or charge distance by the result until the end of the phase. Units with the FLY keyword are not affected.

2CP — EVER VIGILANT
Adeptus Custodes Stratagem

They are the Emperor's own vigilance. They see all.

Use this Stratagem immediately after your opponent sets up a unit that is arriving on the battlefield as reinforcements within 12" of an ADEPTUS CUSTODES INFANTRY unit from your army. That unit can immediately shoot at the enemy unit as if it were the Shooting phase, but you must subtract 1 from all the resulting hit rolls.

3CP — VEXILLA TELEPORT HOMER
Adeptus Custodes Stratagem

Custodes vexillas incorporate sophisticated teleport homers, allowing daring strikes into the heart of the enemy army.

Use this Stratagem at the end of your Movement phase. When you set up a teleporting ADEPTUS CUSTODES unit at the end of the phase, you can set it up wholly within 6" of a friendly VEXILUS PRAETOR (other than one that was set up in this turn) and more than 3" from enemy models. Any models that cannot be set up this way are destroyed.

1CP/3CP — OPEN THE VAULTS
Adeptus Custodes Stratagem

In dire need, the warriors of the Adeptus Custodes bear into battle weapons not used since the siege of the Imperial Palace.

Use this Stratagem before the battle. Your army can have one extra Relic of Terra for 1 CP, or two extra Relics of Terra for 3 CPs. All of the Relics of Terra that you include must be different and be given to different ADEPTUS CUSTODES CHARACTERS. You can only use this Stratagem once per battle.

1CP — AVATARS OF THE EMPEROR
Adeptus Custodes Stratagem

The sight of the Emperor's vengeance embodied and unleashed on the foe is enough to steel the resolve of the most beleaguered armies.

Use this Stratagem at the beginning of the Morale phase. Choose an ADEPTUS CUSTODES unit from your army (other than a VEHICLE). You can use that unit's Leadership characteristic when taking Morale tests for friendly IMPERIUM units within 6" of that unit in this phase.

SHOULDER THE MANTLE
1CP

Adeptus Custodes Stratagem

Should the leader of an Adeptus Custodes army fall, a worthy comrade always stands ready to take his place.

Use this Stratagem when your Warlord is slain. Choose a **SHIELD-CAPTAIN** on the battlefield from your army. They become your Warlord – choose or generate a Warlord Trait for them immediately. For the purposes of the mission, your Warlord is not considered to have been slain while this model is on the battlefield.

BURST MISSILE NET
1CP

Adeptus Custodes Stratagem

Vertus Praetors are experts at lacing the skies with inescapable webs of flakk detonations.

Use this Stratagem in your Shooting phase, when choosing a unit of Vertus Praetors from your army to make their ranged attacks. If they all fire flakkburst missiles at the same target with the **FLY** keyword, you can re-roll failed wound rolls for these attacks.

NETWORKED MACHINE SPIRITS
1CP

Adeptus Custodes Stratagem

The machine spirits of the Adeptus Custodes' Land Raiders can be networked to provide almost supernatural accuracy.

Use this Stratagem in your Shooting phase. Choose a Venerable Land Raider from your army and at least one other friendly Venerable Land Raider within 6" of that model. None of the chosen models suffer any penalties to their hit rolls until the end of the phase.

SPARK OF DIVINITY
1CP

Adeptus Custodes Stratagem

The spark of divinity within every Custodian can sometimes unravel the sorcerous manifestations of the enemy.

Use this Stratagem when an enemy **PSYKER** manifests a psychic power within 12" of an **ADEPTUS CUSTODES INFANTRY** or **ADEPTUS CUSTODES BIKER** unit from your army. You can take a Deny the Witch test for that unit as if it were a **PSYKER**.

INDOMITABLE GUARDIANS
1CP

Adeptus Custodes Stratagem

Once they have their objective, the warriors of the Adeptus Custodes will not be moved.

Use this Stratagem in your opponent's Fight phase after an enemy unit that charged has fought. Choose an **ADEPTUS CUSTODES** unit from your army that is within 3" of an objective marker and fight with it next.

PLANT THE VEXILLA
1CP

Adeptus Custodes Stratagem

When a Vexilus Praetor plants their vexilla in the ground, they can project the power of the ancient standard even further.

Use this Stratagem at the end of your Movement phase. Choose a **VEXILUS PRAETOR** from your army that did not move in that phase. You can increase the range of the Custodes Vexilla ability for that model by 6" until your next Movement phase. The **VEXILUS PRAETOR** that you chose cannot charge this turn.

INSPIRE FEAR
1CP

Adeptus Custodes Stratagem

To see the lions of the Emperor in all of their battle fury is to see one's death, inevitable and swift approaching.

Use this Stratagem at the beginning of the Morale phase. Choose one of your **ADEPTUS CUSTODES** units (other than a **VEHICLE**). Your opponent must add 1 to Morale tests taken for enemy units within 3" of that unit in this phase.

PIERCING STRIKE
1CP

Adeptus Custodes Stratagem

Placing their spear blows perfectly, the Custodians pierce armour joints and vital systems to slay enemy war engines.

Use this Stratagem when you select an **ADEPTUS CUSTODES** unit from your army to attack in the Fight phase. Add 1 to wound rolls made for that unit's guardian spears until the end of the phase.

SENTINEL STORM
2CP

Adeptus Custodes Stratagem

The Custodians fire their bolt casters point-blank into their foes even as they swing their sentinel blades, a lethal technique that only such skilled warriors could employ.

Use this Stratagem at the end of your opponent's Shooting phase. Choose one of your **ADEPTUS CUSTODES** units that is within 1" of an enemy unit. The unit you chose can shoot with its sentinel blades as if it were your Shooting phase.

INESCAPABLE VENGEANCE
2CP

Adeptus Custodes Stratagem

The Allarus Custodians are single-minded when they have their target in their sight.

Use this Stratagem when you select a unit of Allarus Custodians from your army to make their attacks in the Shooting phase. They can target enemy **CHARACTERS** with their attacks, even if they are not the closest enemy model.

WISDOM OF THE ANCIENTS
1CP

Adeptus Custodes Stratagem

The Dreadnoughts of the Adeptus Custodes have seen millennia of war, and can guide their comrades with their wisdom.

Use this Stratagem at the start of any phase. Select an **Adeptus Custodes Dreadnought** from your army. Until the end of the phase, you can re-roll hit rolls of 1 for friendly **Adeptus Custodes** units within 6" of it.

CASTELLAN STRIKE
1CP

Adeptus Custodes Stratagem

The arcing strike of a castellan axe can be all but inescapable, and can hack open weak spots for other blades to exploit.

Use this Stratagem when you select one of your **Adeptus Custodes** units to attack in the Fight phase. As long as more than one model in the unit is attacking with a castellan axe, and they all target the same unit, improve the AP of that unit's castellan axes to -3 until the end of the phase.

CONCUSSION GRENADES
1CP

Adeptus Custodes Stratagem

With the press of a rune, the balistus grenade launcher can switch to firing archeotech rounds designed to incapacitate.

Use this Stratagem in your Shooting phase, when choosing a unit of Allarus Custodians from your army to attack. Until the end of the phase, their balistus grenade launchers have an AP characteristic of 0, and **Infantry** units that are hit by these attacks are stunned until the end of the turn – they cannot fire Overwatch and your opponent must subtract 1 from hit rolls made for the unit.

EYES OF THE EMPEROR
1CP

Adeptus Custodes Stratagem

The Adeptus Custodes strike suddenly, guided by intelligence offered by the Eyes of the Emperor.

Use this Stratagem when you generate a Tactical Objective. You can discard that Tactical Objective immediately and generate a new Tactical Objective.

VICTOR OF THE BLOOD GAMES
2CP

Adeptus Custodes Stratagem

What foe can withstand a warrior who has overcome the defences of Holy Terra itself?

Use this Stratagem when you set up an **Adeptus Custodes Character** from your army during deployment. You can re-roll one hit roll, one wound roll or one save roll for this model in each turn.

EVEN IN DEATH…
2CP

Adeptus Custodes Stratagem

Even to their last breath, the heroic warriors of the Adeptus Custodes continue to fight on against those who would oppose the Master of Mankind.

Use this Stratagem when an **Adeptus Custodes Character** from your army is slain. Before removing the model from the battlefield, it can immediately either shoot as if it were the Shooting phase, or fight as if it were the Fight phase.

AVENGE THE FALLEN
1CP

Adeptus Custodes Stratagem

The loss of a Custodian is commemorated by the tolling of the Bell of Lost Souls on Terra, and by their comrades' bloody vengeance on the battlefield.

Use this Stratagem when you select an **Adeptus Custodes** unit from your army to attack in the Fight phase. Until the end of the phase, increase the Attacks characteristic of each model in the unit by 1 for each model from that unit that was slain this turn.

BRINGERS OF THE EMPEROR'S JUSTICE
1CP

Adeptus Custodes Stratagem

The Adeptus Custodes have never forgiven the Traitor Legions for their part in Horus' rebellion. Whenever the chance arises, they exact vengeance with lethal efficiency.

Use this Stratagem when an **Adeptus Custodes** unit from your army is chosen to attack in the Fight phase. Each time you make a hit roll of 6+ for a model in that unit during this phase, it can, if it was targeting a **Heretic Astartes** unit, immediately make an extra attack against the same unit using the same weapon. If it was targeting a **Black Legion** unit, it instead makes an extra attack on a hit roll of 4+. These extra attacks cannot themselves generate any further attacks.

STOOPING DIVE
3CP

Adeptus Custodes Stratagem

Guided by their predictive auguries and centuries of combat experience, the Vertus Praetors excel at swooping down to intercept threats the moment they manifest themselves.

Use this Stratagem at the end of your opponent's Charge phase. Choose an **Adeptus Custodes Biker** unit from your army that is within 12" of an enemy unit. You can declare a charge with that unit as if it were your Charge phase. If the unit's charge is successful, that unit fights before all other units in the subsequent Fight phase – even before charging units. If your opponent has any units with similar abilities, take it in turns to resolve them, beginning with your opponent.

RELICS OF TERRA

During the Great Crusade, the Custodians hoarded some of the most powerful and esoteric weapons technology ever encountered by the Imperium. Though much of it was expended during the Horus Heresy, some of these ancient artefacts still exist, locked away in vaults deep beneath the Imperial Palace, waiting to be borne to war when the need is greatest.

If your army is led by an Adeptus Custodes Warlord, you may give one of the following Relics of Terra to an **ADEPTUS CUSTODES CHARACTER** in your army. Named characters such as Captain-General Trajann Valoris cannot be given any of the following relics – they have their own unique wargear.

Note that some weapons replace one of the model's existing weapons. Where this is the case, you must, if you are playing a matched play game or are otherwise using points values, still pay the cost of the weapon that is being replaced. Write down any Relics of Terra your characters have on your army roster.

GATEKEEPER

This potent weapon thrums with barely contained power. Its machine spirits are capable of near-prescient predictive targeting, allowing the wielder to mow down the enemy before they can come within blade's reach.

Model with a guardian spear only. The Gatekeeper replaces the model's guardian spear and has the following profile:

WEAPON	RANGE	TYPE	S	AP	D
Gatekeeper (shooting)	24"	Rapid Fire 3	4	-1	2
Gatekeeper (melee)	Melee	Melee	+1	-3	D3

Abilities: Overwatch attacks made with this weapon successfully hit on rolls of 3+ rather than 6.

RAIMENT OF SORROWS

Handwoven by the sisters of the Order of Lamentations and allowed to sit in state at the foot of the Golden Throne for a full century, this shroud-like raiment is a potent reminder of the Custodians' one great defeat. Its presence fills them with a cold determination to never fail again.

Roll a D6 each time a friendly **ADEPTUS CUSTODES INFANTRY** or **BIKER** model is destroyed within 6" of the bearer, before removing the model as a casualty. On a 4+ that model musters one last surge of strength before succumbing to its wounds; it can either shoot with one of its weapons as if it were the Shooting phase, or make a single attack as if it were the Fight phase. You cannot use the Even in Death… Stratagem on a model that does so.

EAGLE'S EYE

This magnificent helm incorporates sensorium-gheists, trapped within micro-reliquaries and compelled to shriek their technomantic warnings to the wearer whenever danger threatens.

Improve this model's invulnerable save by 1 (to a maximum of 3+).

AURIC AQUILAS

Incorporating forbidden secrets of ancient archeotech from the Dark Age of Technology, Auric Aquilas is a truly magnificent gravitic jetbike. Swift as thought and protected by a shimmering golden force field, it bears its rider swiftly and safely into battle.

BIKER model only. This model has a 3+ invulnerable save. In addition, you can re-roll failed charge rolls made for this model.

THE PRAETORIAN PLATE

This suit of Allarus Terminator armour – itself a handcrafted relic of great antiquity – has been adapted to incorporate a still more ancient empyric beacon and archeotech teleport-shunter that allows its wearer to leap directly through the warp to the aid of those he is sworn to defend.

TERMINATOR model only. When you set the bearer up, choose a friendly **IMPERIUM CHARACTER**. At the end of your opponent's Charge phase, if there is an enemy model within 1" of that character, you can remove the bearer from the battlefield (if they are on the battlefield) and, even if they were not on the battlefield, set them up within 3" of that character and within 1" of an enemy model. The bearer is not considered to have charged.

THE VEILED BLADE

An ancient blade that burns with a bitterly cold and dark energy, the Veiled Blade is bestowed upon a Custodian who has vowed to recover that which should remain hidden from Humanity and return it to the Dark Cells.

Model with a sentinel blade only. The Veiled Blade replaces the model's sentinel blade and has the following profile:

WEAPON	RANGE	TYPE	S	AP	D
Veiled Blade (shooting)	12"	Pistol 2	4	0	1
Veiled Blade (melee)	Melee	Melee	User	-3	D3

Abilities: Each time the bearer fights whilst they are within 3" of an objective marker, they can make 2 additional attacks with this weapon.

EMPEROR'S LIGHT

Said to have been crafted from a crystallised shard of the Emperor's glorious light, this masterwork misericordia has been borne into battle by three separate Captain-Generals. It is said to flood the heart of its victim with holy radiance, and is an object of dread to traitors and heretics alike.

Model with a misericordia only. The Emperor's Light replaces the model's misericordia and has the following profile:

WEAPON	RANGE	TYPE	S	AP	D
Emperor's Light	Melee	Melee	User	-2	1

Abilities: Each time the bearer fights, it can make 1 additional attack with this weapon unless it is also equipped with a storm shield. In addition, add 1 to any Morale tests taken by enemy units within 12" of the bearer.

WRATH ANGELIS

This ancient and expertly crafted vexilla was created for the battle against the Orks upon the world of Ullanor. During that conflict, pinpoint fire support was key to victory. Thus, this vexilla incorporates a multi-spectral targeting shrine that links to warships in orbit and guides in trans-atmospheric strikes with remarkable accuracy.

Model with a Vexilla Magnifica only. The Wrath Angelis replaces that model's vexilla: it loses the Custodes Vexilla ability. Instead, friendly **IMPERIUM INFANTRY** and **BIKER** units within 6" of the bearer in the Morale phase automatically pass Morale tests, and once per battle in your Movement phase, if the bearer does not move, you can roll a D6 for each unit (friend or foe) within 6". Subtract 1 from the result if the unit being rolled for is a **CHARACTER**, or 2 from the result if the unit being rolled for is **ADEPTUS CUSTODES**. On a 4+ the unit being rolled for suffers D3 mortal wounds.

AURIC SHACKLES

These fetters were forged in the Dark Age of Technology, and adapt themselves to shut down the neural nets of any sentient beings, rendering even the thought of escape impossible. They are used to capture the Imperium's most dangerous foes.

Your opponent must subtract 1 from the Attacks characteristic of enemy **CHARACTERS** whilst they are within 6" of the bearer (to a minimum of 1). In addition, in missions that use victory points, if the bearer slays the enemy Warlord in the Fight phase, you score an additional D3 victory points.

OBLITERATUM

This dread vambrace weapon incorporates several forbidden technologies whose possession would be death to any beyond the Adeptus Custodes. It fires concentrated antimatter, compressed within splinterglass canisters that shatter upon impact. Victims are annihilated on a molecular level by the night-black blasts caused by this weapon's fire, vanishing in terrifying eruptions of nothingness.

Model with a balistus grenade launcher only. The Obliteratum replaces the model's balistus grenade launcher and has the following profile:

WEAPON	RANGE	TYPE	S	AP	D
Obliteratum	12"	Assault 1	10	-4	D3

FULMINARIS AGGRESSOR

This vexilla was fashioned after the fall of Goge Vandire to honour the wrath of the Emperor in punishing traitors and tyrants. Its micro-thundercoil generatorum crackles with barely restrained power that arcs out to annihilate nearby foes.

Model with a Vexilla Defensor only. The Fulminaris Aggressor replaces that model's vexilla: it loses the Custodes Vexilla ability. Instead, friendly **IMPERIUM INFANTRY** and **BIKER** units within 6" of the bearer in the Morale phase automatically pass Morale tests, and the Fulminaris Aggressor has the following weapon profile:

WEAPON	RANGE	TYPE	S	AP	D
Fulminaris Aggressor (shooting)	8"	Assault D6	4	-1	1
Fulminaris Aggressor (melee)	Melee	Melee	+2	-1	1

Abilities: Attacks made with this weapon's shooting profile automatically hit.

THE CASTELLAN'S MARK

This finely worked pauldron is awarded to whichever living Custodian currently holds the greatest tally of victories in the Blood Games. It is rare, of course, that even the resourceful warriors of the Adeptus Custodes succeed in these endeavours, and so to honour one who has done so more times than any other is only right. He who bears the Castellan's Mark is guaranteed to be a superlative strategic genius, an expert in spotting and exploiting weaknesses with merciless efficiency.

If the bearer is on the battlefield, at the beginning of the game but before the first turn you can remove them and up to one friendly **ADEPTUS CUSTODES** unit within 6" of them from the battlefield and set them up again following the mission rules. You must set them up on the battlefield.

FAITH ABSOLUTE

This ominous vexilla was created for the infamous Witching Wars. It is able to discharge a pulse of disruptive contra-empyric energies that can unmake an onrushing psychic manifestation in a heartbeat.

Model with a Vexilla Magnifica only. The Faith Absolute replaces that model's vexilla: it loses the Custodes Vexilla ability. Instead, friendly **IMPERIUM INFANTRY** and **BIKER** units within 6" of the bearer in the Morale phase automatically pass Morale tests, and the bearer can attempt to deny one psychic power in each enemy Psychic phase as if they were a **PSYKER**.

'Whatever the weapons we wield, whatever the deeds we perform, they are justified. Without us, the Golden Throne would fall, and without the Emperor to guide them, Humanity would follow.'

- Ganestus Talorn, Allarus Custodian

WARLORD TRAITS

Those Custodians that lead their brethren into battle are amongst the most accomplished warriors in the entire Imperium. Their mastery of strategy, tactics and every aspect of combat are second to none.

If the Warlord of your army is an **ADEPTUS CUSTODES CHARACTER**, you can pick their Warlord Trait from the Adeptus Custodes Warlord Traits table, or roll a D6 and consult the table to generate their Warlord Trait.

D6 RESULT

1 CHAMPION OF THE IMPERIUM

This Warlord is amongst the finest champions in the entire Imperium, and their presence inspires all nearby to acts of heroism.

Friendly **ADEPTUS CUSTODES INFANTRY**, **BIKER** and **DREADNOUGHT** units that are within 12" of your Warlord at the start of your opponent's Charge phase can make Heroic Interventions this phase in the same manner as **CHARACTERS**.

2 PEERLESS WARRIOR

With every masterful strike and artful parry, this Warlord proves himself the master of one-to-one combat against even the most terrible foes.

Each time you make a hit roll of 6+ for your Warlord in the Fight phase, they can immediately make an extra attack against the same unit using the same weapon. These extra attacks cannot themselves generate any further attacks.

3 SUPERIOR CREATION

The cellular alchemy that went into the creation of this heroic warrior rendered him breathtakingly resilient.

Each time your Warlord loses a wound, roll a D6; on a 5+ your Warlord does not lose that wound.

4 IMPREGNABLE MIND

No blandishment or invasion by the enemy can overcome the fortress of this Warlord's mind, and his strength of will can crush that of lesser beings.

Your Warlord can attempt to Deny the Witch once in each of your opponent's Psychic phases as if they were a **PSYKER**. When they do so, add 1 to the result of the Deny the Witch test.

5 RADIANT MANTLE

The holy light of the Emperor himself glows around this magnificent warrior in a sublime halo. Enemies are blinded by its glory, forced to recoil in pain and terror.

Your opponent must subtract 1 from hit rolls that target your Warlord.

6 EMPEROR'S COMPANION

As a member of the Adeptus Custodes' inner circle, this Warlord is amongst the deadliest of his order.

You can re-roll the dice for the damage inflicted by your Warlord's attacks.

NAMED CHARACTERS AND WARLORD TRAITS

The Captain-General of the Adeptus Custodes is renowned for his methodology as much as for his deeds on the battlefield. If he is your Warlord, he must be given the associated Warlord Trait shown below.

NAMED CHARACTER	WARLORD TRAIT
Captain-General Trajann Valoris	Champion of the Imperium

POINTS VALUES

If you are playing a matched play game, or a game that uses a points limit, you can use the following lists to determine the total points cost of your army. Simply add together the points values of all your models, as well as the weapons and wargear they are equipped with, to determine your army's total points value.

UNITS

UNIT	MODELS PER UNIT	POINTS PER MODEL (Does not include wargear)
Allarus Custodians	3-10	70
Custodian Guard	3-10	40
Custodian Wardens	3-10	49
Shield-Captain	1	110
Shield-Captain in Allarus Terminator Armour	1	130
Shield-Captain on Dawneagle Jetbike	1	150
Venerable Contemptor Dreadnought	1	130
Venerable Land Raider	1	283
Vertus Praetors	3-10	80
Vexilus Praetor	1	80
Vexilus Praetor in Allarus Terminator Armour	1	100

NAMED CHARACTERS

UNIT	MODELS PER UNIT	POINTS PER MODEL (Includes wargear)
Captain-General Trajann Valoris	1	250

RANGED WEAPONS

WEAPON	POINTS PER WEAPON
Balistus grenade launcher	0
Castellan axe	14
Combi-bolter	2
Guardian spear	12
Hunter-killer missile	6
Hurricane bolter	10
Kheres-pattern assault cannon	25
Multi-melta	27
Salvo launcher	25
Sentinel blade	9
Storm bolter	2
Twin heavy bolter	17
Twin lascannon	50

MELEE WEAPONS

WEAPON	POINTS PER WEAPON
Dreadnought combat weapon	40
Interceptor lance	0
Misericordia	4

OTHER WARGEAR

WARGEAR	POINTS PER ITEM
Storm shield (CHARACTERS)	15
Storm shield (other models)	10
Vexilla Defensor	20
Vexilla Imperius	50
Vexilla Magnifica	30

TACTICAL OBJECTIVES

The Adeptus Custodes engage in battles that would leave lesser armies in ruin. They seize victory in the Emperor's name when no one else can, and prove their absolute supremacy over their enemies with every perfectly placed shot, every killing blade-stroke, and every crushing conquest they achieve.

If your army is led by an **ADEPTUS CUSTODES** Warlord, these Tactical Objectives replace the Capture and Control Tactical Objectives (numbers 11-16) in the *Warhammer 40,000* rulebook. If a mission uses Tactical Objectives, players use the normal rules for using Tactical Objectives with the following exception: when an Adeptus Custodes player generates a Capture and Control objective (numbers 11-16), they instead generate the corresponding Adeptus Custodes Tactical Objective, as shown below. Other Tactical Objectives (numbers 21-66) are generated normally.

D66	TACTICAL OBJECTIVE
11	Deliver Victory
12	Eliminate Threats
13	War Zone Secure
14	Keep Them At Spear's Length
15	Crush Their Resistance
16	The Emperor's Vengeance

11 — DELIVER VICTORY — *Adeptus Custodes*

Victory for the Adeptus Custodes inevitably has far-reaching ramifications for the entire Imperium.

Score 1 victory point at the end of your turn if you score at least 1 victory point from another Tactical Objective in your turn.

12 — ELIMINATE THREATS — *Adeptus Custodes*

The Ten Thousand only deploy when a threat is so great that it could directly bring harm to the throneworld itself. When such dangers are eliminated, it is cause for great celebration.

Score 1 victory point at the end of your turn if at least one enemy unit was destroyed in your turn. If three or more enemy units were destroyed in your turn, score D3 victory points instead.

13 — WAR ZONE SECURE — *Adeptus Custodes*

Some dangers to the Golden Throne are so great that entire war zones must be mercilessly controlled in order to find and neutralise them.

Score 1 victory point at the end of your turn if you hold at least three objective markers.

14 — KEEP THEM AT SPEAR'S LENGTH — *Adeptus Custodes*

The Adeptus Custodes trust no one beyond their own ranks, for all others are fallible. They keep allies and enemies alike at a distance of two spear lengths.

Score 1 victory point at the end of your turn if there are no other units within 3" of **ADEPTUS CUSTODES** units from your army (with the exception of other friendly **ADEPTUS CUSTODES** units). You cannot score this objective in your first turn.

15 — CRUSH THEIR RESISTANCE — *Adeptus Custodes*

No matter the odds they face, the Adeptus Custodes can seize victory from even the most desperate strategic situation.

When you generate this Tactical Objective, your opponent chooses an objective marker. Score D3 victory points at the end of the turn if you control this objective marker.

16 — THE EMPEROR'S VENGEANCE — *Adeptus Custodes*

The Adeptus Custodes advance swiftly and crush their enemies with uncompromising ferocity.

Score D3 victory points if you control an objective marker that was controlled by your opponent at the start of the turn. If you control three or more objective markers that were controlled by your opponent at the start of the turn, score D3+3 victory points instead.

'Remember what we fight for, my comrades. The sanctity and safety of the Golden Throne itself, the safety of the very Master of Mankind, relies upon our victory here this day. Now raise your spears, gird your minds and souls, and let us banish these vile Daemons so that we may once more say we did our duty.'

- Captain-General Trajann Valoris, before the Battle of Lion's Gate